JENNIFER STARNS

The Two Kingdoms

A simple way to view our complex world

First published by Platypus Publishing 2023

Copyright © 2023 by Jennifer Starns

All rights reserved. No part of this publication may be reproduced, stored or transmitted in any form or by any means, electronic, mechanical, photocopying, recording, scanning, or otherwise without written permission from the publisher. It is illegal to copy this book, post it to a website, or distribute it by any other means without permission.

Jennifer Starns asserts the moral right to be identified as the author of this work.

Jennifer Starns has no responsibility for the persistence or accuracy of URLs for external or third-party Internet Websites referred to in this publication and does not guarantee that any content on such Websites is, or will remain, accurate or appropriate.

Designations used by companies to distinguish their products are often claimed as trademarks. All brand names and product names used in this book and on its cover are trade names, service marks, trademarks and registered trademarks of their respective owners. The publishers and the book are not associated with any product or vendor mentioned in this book. None of the companies referenced within the book have endorsed the book.

First edition

ISBN: 978-1-959555-87-2

This book was professionally typeset on Reedsy.
Find out more at reedsy.com

To my most favorite people, Julian and Jakob. What gifts you are, to reflect back to me who I am, and to generously engage me while I learn to parent. You have shown me how to play and struggle well, within the light of unconditional love, grace, and forgiveness. I am inspired by your kind hearts, sense of adventure, and creativity. I love you!

'Trust in the Lord with all your heart and lean not on your own understanding. In all your ways submit to Him, and He will direct Your path.'

Contents

Acknowledgement	iii
INTRODUCTION	1
Chapter 1: How it Started	5
Chapter 2: Earthlings' Current Dilemma	8
Chapter 3: The Two Kingdoms – Structure	14
Chapter 4: The Two Kingdoms – Secrets	22
Chapter 5: The Two Kingdoms – Rule on Earth	25
Chapter 6: The Two Kingdoms – Declaration of War	30
Chapter 7: The Two Kingdoms – History	33
Chapter 8: The Plan – Kingdom of Light	37
Chapter 9: The Plan – Kingdom of Darkness	42
Chapter 10: The Plan – Human Efforts	45
Chapter 11: The War Operation	55
Chapter 12: Human Systems and Operations	59
Chapter 13: The Human Tendencies	65
Chapter 14: The Solution to the Human Condition	70
Chapter 15: Understanding Life Versus Religious Dogma	77
Chapter 16: Q&A Using the Two Kingdom Framework	80
Chapter 17: Interpreting our World through the Two Kingdoms	86
Chapter 18: Notable Battles in Play	90
Chapter 19: War Preparation & Assisting the War Effort	93
Chapter 20: The Source	98
APPENDIX: Status of War Operations	102
RESOURCES	106

Notes	108
About the Author	114

Acknowledgement

Decades of excellent books, sermons, and conversations have seeped into my subconscious, so I'm not entirely sure how anything I write could accurately be attributed solely to me.

As I hope to convey clearly through this book, God[1] is sovereign over all; I am humbled and grateful He chose to include me in His work. This book is an act of worship and obedience to Him.

I sincerely thank all the humans who joined or encouraged me on this book journey. I am grateful for the various communities that supported and shared life with me – friends, family, and coworkers. Those who allowed me space to live and process aloud thoughts, ideas, observations, and life lessons. The list of names would require its own book, so I've trimmed the list to those who were aware of this book and helped or encouraged me to publish it.

Special thanks to Cheryl Hylton, Dionne Brown, Joan Brokalis, Karin Koek, Kathy Riffer, Michael Barnett, Renee Brauns, and Robert Jackson.

The Lord bless you and keep you; the Lord make His face shine upon you, and be gracious to you; the Lord lift up His countenance upon you, and give you peace.[2]

INTRODUCTION

The road to writing this book is the intersection of many paths. One path was the desire to connect meaningfully with my family of origin. I didn't grow up in a typical family with a mother, father, and siblings. Though I'm from a big family, we didn't do life together. I longed and believed we could achieve more if we lived closer or connected more meaningfully.

At the same time, I was seeing strange things and wondered if others were seeing the same. The world looked chaotic, but I suspected chaos was only at the lower levels - the level of ordinary people. A few people were open to engaging me in conversation, but I didn't want to overwhelm any one person, so I had to divide the conversations among a few.

I started drawing what I saw, then added words and explanations. I found myself writing more and more. I had a fleeting thought that I should write a book, but that didn't make sense. I'm not a writer. I love to read, but writing a book is a whole different story.

Writing has never been my thing. In high school, I focused on natural sciences. I like being brief. I prefer working with numbers. It's exact and not prone to misinterpretation. You are either right or wrong. I knew when I arrived at the answer. In writing, I don't know when enough is enough, or if I am close to the answer.

Writing long essays exhausts my energy. Throughout my career,

I preferred using bulleted lists, diagrams, and tables to convey my ideas. You'll see what I mean in this book. I figure there's something pathological about this mindset, but that's for another time.

What I saw in society triggered questions about this world. It looked complex, but I figured there was an uncomplicated answer. I approached it as I would a complex algebraic equation or a complex computer system. A complex computer system is sophisticated by nature; however, the best ones are also simple at the user level. If it is complicated, no one will use it, and it would be useless.

I started with a list of major systems that affect us – economic, educational, religious, political, and so on. I continued to zoom out until I reached the simplest and highest level. I simplified this complex equation and arrived at a theoretical expression, $x=2$. The systems pointed to two kingdoms.

My son told me, consultants solve problems, and since I've been a consultant for so long, I'm always seeing problems to solve. I agreed. Reluctantly. Now, when I see a problem or issue, I learn to slow down and spend more time questioning myself. Do I also have that problem? Is it a problem for me to solve? Is it necessary for me to say something?

What does that have to do with my family? Because they are family members. It's not like work, this is close to home. I don't know everyone yet and to the same extent. We have the potential to see each other – warts and all. How can I show up for them in a cooperative manner, and not dictate solutions? How can I see their issues, without pointing them out? How can they help me with my issues without me feeling defensive?

How do I give them what I have so they can continue to build on it, without appearing as Ms. Know-it-all or a savior? But I didn't want to die without passing on all I've learned and acquired – the good, bad, and indifferent.

An autobiography seemed premature and self-centered, and I was

INTRODUCTION

concerned that too much of it would be about me, and they'd miss the message. I wasn't confident I could explain what I've done or was done to me, in a way that is beneficial to them. So, I wanted to explain what I critically believe and value, because they inform my positive outcomes.

Maybe I should write a book. That thought came from nowhere.

I didn't tell a soul because I couldn't believe it myself. Then I had a conversation with a friend, she started, "I am reading a book. It's by an author who is not a theologian. She is writing about her experience with God. It reads like how I would expect your book to sound if you wrote a book." I was shocked!

I confessed to her; I was thinking of writing a book. We laughed. I decided to write the book.

I handwrote 22 pages across 3 days. But then I didn't like the tone; it sounded preachy. It wasn't a total loss though; it became my proof of concept – I could write a long script.

I started to write to my family, then it morphed into a book addressed to me. I was reading the book I was writing and found myself crying as I read. The book was for me as for anyone else. I found that what I believed and how I lived were not in alignment, and I was devastated. But I was elated at the same time. This was an opportunity for me to grow. I may sell only two copies. That's fine because I received so much life from the process.

I didn't know how to publish a book, so I first signed up with a publishing company. The plan was to meet weekly across 12 months. Then I met Punchy Books and switched. Punchy Books promised I could write and publish a short book within 90 days. I liked that, I figured that was short enough to get it done and not change my mind.

In that program, "by chance" I met my accountability partner who was on a similar journey, writing a book for the first time, about Jesus[3].

We both love reading books. We don't like books padded with fluff - we don't care to read through 100 pages before getting to the heart of the book.

We believe non-fiction should be direct, cut to the chase, and give us the juicy bit from the outset.

Here's one of those books.

Definitions and how to read this book

This book is more of a manifesto. You may gain insight by going directly to any page, however, reading it from the beginning would flow better. I may explain an idea upfront, then use it later without further explanation.

Nonetheless, I've used specific keywords or terms repeatedly. Even though some words are commonly used, I feel it's important for me to explain what I mean. These terms are marked throughout the book and explained at the end as *Notes*.

Chapter 1: How it Started

It started with a video clip:

"...*the big political and economic question of the 21st century will be, what do we need humans for, or at least what do we need so many humans for.*"

...

"*At present, the best guess we have is to keep them happy with drugs and computer games.*"[4]

My mind started to race. What if you were feeling down and depressed, questioning your purpose or existence, then heard this bleak forecast? Wouldn't this deepen your sense of despair, and perhaps lead you to abandon your search for deeper meaning?

Perhaps if it were said in jest or by someone with little to no influence, it wouldn't matter as much. But that was said by Yuval Noah Harari, historian, and professor, advisor to global leaders. We pass laws and make policies using the opinion of people like Dr. Harari. What he says matters.

So, if this mindless use of drugs and computer games is not the optimal future for humans, what is?

The answer lies in the truth about humanity. **Who we really are, our value, and our purpose on earth**. Until we understand our value and purpose, we don't have a standard to measure whether we are doing what we should. Instead, we live on autopilot, trusting whomever we think is in control to tell us what to think and do.

Today's young people are noticing that something is just not adding up. The older generation is working so hard, they haven't got enough time to notice the same. If only we could listen and talk, really talk with each other. We would unite generations skillful at solving problems with generations having insight into identifying problems.

Instead, we are moving away from each other. We are beginning to isolate ourselves to address our problems. It seems like everyone is struggling against something or for something. When the struggle gets too intense, we start to give up. We walk around with our heads held down, our shoulders slumped, and our faces devoid of emotion. We are hurting but say we're okay.

If work and pleasure were the whole point of human existence, we would have given up long ago. But we haven't because we sense that we have a purpose beyond our materialistic world. And hope to get there.

Physical pleasure and work, though they account for much of our focus throughout our lives, do not define our human value. Other humans or our possessions do not determine our value. To imply that playing computer games and taking drugs is the best we can strive for, gives the impression that humans are no more than biological matter. The creator of humans may want to weigh in on this gross devaluation.

Take children, for example, they didn't choose to be born. A priceless value is assigned to them by healthy parents. A bully on the playground may assign whatever value they believe to that child. However, that doesn't mean the bully is right. If that bully dares to harm that child, the parent **must** intervene.

Humans also have a Creator who has already assigned a value to us. The value is not based on human standards but on what He will pay for us. This Creator will also determine how we'll end. Ultimately human existence will pretty much wrap up the same way we started - **without human permission.**

CHAPTER 1: HOW IT STARTED

I started writing this as a personal letter to my family, the younger generation. However, I quickly found that I was also writing to myself. Even when I say "you."

So, what I am putting forward are the thoughts and observations of a family member and not those of an academic, theologian, or writer.

Chapter 2: Earthlings' Current Dilemma

"The human spirit can endure a sick body, but who can bear a crushed spirit?"[5]

Today, we face so many issues simultaneously or in quick succession. Personal concerns such as **job** security, making **enough money**, saving enough money for the future, and having enough money for basic needs. Taking care of **health** and housing, educational opportunities. To **help** others. We want to know how to handle our **relationships** well – our parents, children, spouses, coworkers, employers, employees, and family friends. The best approach for connecting with "**friends**" on social media. Taking care of one's **body**, staying healthy, and being attractive. Taking care of our **spiritual** life. Having **fun**. Meeting **obligations** and keeping promises. How can we feel **happy** all the time? Why can't our emotions be at one consistent high level?

While handling these issues, our smartphone notifications and media are demanding that we invite more issues into our lives:

War, Racism, Abortion, LGBT, Illegal Immigration, Transgenderism, Economic Instability, People and Institutional Failures, and Pop Culture.

The fear of being left out demands you keep up to date with the latest "news." But we still have only 24 hours within a day, 7 days within a week.

While all this is bombarding us 24/7, our bodies and psyche have

CHAPTER 2: EARTHLINGS' CURRENT DILEMMA

been traumatized, and our stamina depleted. Over the last 20 years, we have experienced:

- Y2K doom predictions
- The 9/11 Attack
- Missing Airplanes
- Wars
- 2008 Economic Recession
- Intense political divisions played out *ad nauseum.*
- Major natural disasters – Earthquakes, Hurricanes, Tsunamis, Tornadoes, Floods
- Mass School Shootings
- Riots and Protests in the streets
- COVID-19 Pandemic and the ensuing fall-out
- Death of prominent world figures, such as Nelson Mandela, Kobe Bryant, Queen of England

No one can blame you if you feel exhausted with little stamina left in your tank.

Fear is all around. People are afraid of saying the wrong thing or picking the wrong side. Without being financially independent, you might feel your job is at stake if you say the wrong thing.

At ground level, we tend to follow blindly and sincerely whatever we are taught, what to value or devalue. Sometimes our personal values conflict with others. Depending on the strength of our conviction and character, we may give into the values of others to the detriment of our own souls. Or, the opposition is so debilitating, it's much easier to go with the flow. When we glimpse the contradiction, we dismiss it and move along, not questioning. We behave as if it were supposed to be different, then someone else would do something about it. You might not believe you have the power to make a difference, so you give up your power.

Even if as an individual, we were not severely affected by these events, the plight of others or the knowledge of these events has harmed us emotionally. So, how should we live so we remain strong and resilient? What can we do to make it better for the next generations?

It's how we think of life! It's the image we have in our heads and hearts when we think of ourselves, others, and the world. We can see how everything falls into place if we get the true image.

Our Image of Life

Everyone has an image of life. It's a framework we use to make sense of and set standards for life. When we experience life, and it aligns with our image, we find it acceptable, and our emotions are positive or neutral. When we experience a life counter to this image, our emotions turn negative.

The image I am proposing we adopt is the Truth about life. It's an image of stable life that agrees with what we know to be true - and flexible with what we don't know. For example, there are parts of yourself you know to be real because you can touch, feel, smell, taste, and see those parts. There are inner parts you might need special equipment like an ultrasound to see better. However, there is a part of us, for which there are no machines developed to "see" – our mind, soul, and spirit. You know, those parts that hurt, and you wish you could take out and soothe, but you can't?

You know you have those many parts, but if you are treated as if you have only physical parts, you might wonder, what about the other parts? Computer games and video may feed **some** parts, but what about the others?

To consider the other parts, which we don't have the machinery to evaluate, means we should investigate the source of these non-tangible parts. What's their purpose? Why do we have them? Who gave them to us?

Where did we get our non-tangible parts?

From our Creator.

We were given a spirit within a physical body. Our spirits were meant to connect to our Creator, and He was meant to direct our lives. But we have all but ignored the fact that we have a spirit and have focused instead on the physical, which has left us lopsided and potentially unbalanced. So, ignoring the Creator and His guidance, we have this world today:

- We don't treat each other as though we're valuable. We've created systems and institutions with hierarchies and groupings, then assigned values through social, political, and economic dogma. Group classification is great for identification but not so much for assigning value.
- We've assigned value to people based on wealth, popularity, appearance, skills, nationality, power, race, profession, social status, and so on.
- We've demeaned people to the point of selling them, murdering them, stealing from them, enslaving them.
- We've classified, corralled, labeled, and sorted people to control where they go, what they do, what they learn, and what they know. **It has become easier to think of humans as avatars rather than invaluable souls – beloved and eternal.**

Within the last few decades, we have witnessed a worldwide shake-up. Most powerful institutions have been hit with a crisis. These shakeups expose vulnerabilities, lies, deceit, and false impressions.

Reports of major scandals, revelations, or failures are reported from all areas: the economy, academia, politics, religion, health, government, entertainment, and workplace, to name a few.

Secrets are kept from the population, and it's assumed to be for good reason. However, with the amount of information being declassified or revealed, what else is hidden from us? What's being hidden that's preventing us from really living? What else are we told to accept as is?

Many people may prefer not to know about this sort of thing. It sounds weird. They'd prefer to leave this with the media to filter and cherry-pick the information we are to focus on. We'd instead follow wherever the masses go[6]. It's less complicated that way.

If that's you, there's no judgment, it's easier, and invites less scrutiny to "go with the program." But do you wonder sometimes:

- Why are people starving when we have enough for everyone in the world to be fed?
- We have a lot of uninhabited lands, so why do we have so many homeless?
- If money can be printed and is not a natural resource, why is it owned by so few? Why do we even need money?
- Why do we hold such opposing values, though we have so much in common?
- What is causing us to feel sad and hopeless, even though we have a lot going for us?
- Why are we so unkind, though we really, really want to be kind?

The answers to these questions are easier understood within the framework of the **Two Kingdoms.**

What is happening now is the unfolding of a story that began at the beginning of time. As we come closer to the end, it's unavoidable that the truth will be revealed.

CHAPTER 2: EARTHLINGS' CURRENT DILEMMA

Having listened to several podcasts and opinion pieces, I've heard some ideas for solving our problems including:

- Create alternate systems to remove power from the few.
- Exercise civil disobedience in response to policies being proposed.
- Curtail the activities of unsavory mindsets and keep individuals who act in unsavory ways from participating in society.
- Prepare for the apocalypse.
- Withdraw and live off the grid.

However, most miss the bigger picture or completely ignore the "elephant in the room." Eventually, there will be an end to every human life on this earth. The Creator started this and will end it. Before we reach that end, each person must decide what happens to their spirit after Earth. Until then, **we can be tricked, manipulated, and deceived to make decisions, act on thoughts that didn't originate from us, and vociferously defend values that were never ours.** This is the proverbial elephant.

What we believe will determine how we handle our responsibility and choices. I want to help simplify this process by drawing attention to the two kingdoms.

Our elected officials, corporate leaders, heads of government, and global elites are not the final authority regarding humanity. It's not our religious leaders, either. The final authority lies with our Creator, through the power and authority he has given to humans, Lucifer, and the gods[7] of this world.

Chapter 3: The Two Kingdoms – Structure

The kingdoms are not of Earth's physical realm; they are spiritual. We cannot use our five senses to observe them. And like earthly kingdoms, spiritual kingdoms have rulers, powers, and jurisdiction. They have control and influence in our physical world and have a greater impact than humans. We'll refer to these kingdoms as the **Kingdom of Light** and the **Kingdom of Darkness**.

Though **Lucifer is powerful and opposes God, he is not the equal and opposite of God.** At most, he is as powerful as a powerful angel of God since that was his position before his fall.

These kingdoms existed before the beginning of human time and are spiritual, they possess these earthly attributes[8]:

CHAPTER 3: THE TWO KINGDOMS – STRUCTURE

Attributes	Kingdom of Light	Kingdom of Darkness
Name	Kingdom Light, Kingdom of Heaven, Kingdom of God	Kingdom of Darkness, Sin
Ruler	God, Jesus Christ, The Holy Spirit	Satan (Lucifer, the devil)
Jurisdiction	Everywhere	Earth
Powers and Authority	God is all-powerful and grants powers to others, including Satan	Satan is powerful, he grants powers to his angels and humans. His powers are extensive, though limited to what God permits.
Subjects or Citizens	Angels and humans who believe and allow God to work through them.	Everyone else – *gods, demons, evil spirits, other humans.*
Population size (Human)	Less than the population of the Kingdom of Darkness.	More than the population of the Kingdom of Light.
Focus	Spiritual Life (Spirit) Contentment Be image-bearers of God (Creative)	Physical Life (Body) Insatiable - Pride, Lust, Passion, Indulge in pleasure, sensuality.
The mission of the ruler	Be in a love relationship with humans as a family.	Kill, steal, and destroy the human spirit to thwart God's plan.
Core Value	Love	Self-centeredness, self-gratification
How the ruler views humans	Human beings are His creation, created in His image and likeness to rule the earth like He does the universe. He values human beings as His creation. He paid for each of us with His blood.	The human is a pawn, used to meet the ruler's goal of defying God. Satan is jealous that God has chosen human beings and made them, in His image, to become His children.
Main Communication	The Word (Bible), thoughts, prayers	Desires, Thoughts, prayers
Result of Obedience	Life = love, joy, peace, patience, kindness, goodness, faithfulness, self-discipline, and so on.	Death = pride, hate, envy, greed, laziness, sexual immorality, gluttony, and so on.

The Two Kingdoms on Earth

By understanding and living in the framework of the Two Kingdoms:

- We'll recognize our individual power and limitations, accept our

responsibilities, and make decisions informed by reality.
- We'll understand ourselves, our motivations, have clarity in what we see, reasons behind our needs, desires, roadblocks, and solutions.
- We'll better understand the why to many of our questions regarding our history, existence, and destination. It explains the reason for the deep desires, our tendencies, as well as reasons for the ironies, contradictions, and paradoxes we observe.
- It will explain why we do what we do and how to live freely.
- We'll better understand why any proper projection on what will become of humans, cannot be answered by humans.

Apart from being real, like gravity, the Two Kingdoms are natural to our world. This concept provides a stable framework to answer and respond to the questions we face regarding ourselves and the environment. It also helps us to understand our past, present, and future. The world and its conflicts will start to make sense.

The concept of the Two Kingdoms is so complete it answers problematic and elusive questions when discussing social, political, religious, economic, or technological topics. Then, when we hear a compelling argument or news, we'll be better able to analyze it honestly and properly and not react with fear and confusion.

As humans, we don't have sufficient knowledge, abilities, skills, or longevity to match those of the spiritual. Seeing so many seeking spiritual enlightenment to break free from human constraints is unsurprising.

- Some have had success with the spiritual realm and have secured "gifts" and "abilities" which enabled them to perform what humans consider as fantastic feats - "meteoric rise in fame and fortune," "magic," "miracles," "supernatural" acts or the stuff of "alien technology."

- Others attempt to break free from human constraints using science and technology.
- Others have worked hard, pressed into their physical abilities, and reaped physical success.
- Still, others struggle to understand how to tap into all or any of these for success.
- It's easy to see why one would believe there are many options, truths, and ways to succeed.

Do you notice we don't have the same definition of "success"? Even worse, in a single transaction, the outcome may mean "success" for one party, but "failure" for another. Here are a few examples:

- Adding unbeneficial substances to our food may produce financial success for the manufacturing company, but would it mean success for the consumer?
- If the employer is stingy and underpays the employees, the employer may be successful, but are the employees?
- Contributing the bare minimum to one's job may be successful for the worker, but what of the employer?
- When burglars steal, they may consider that a success, but what of the victim?
- When the price of housing increases, it is a success for the seller, but what about the buyer?
- When a pandemic occurs, a natural disaster hits, or war is declared, it will be a great opportunity for some, but will it not bring poverty, death, and destruction for others?

Can you think of other examples?

The ideal would be for every party to a transaction to be successful. Do you believe human beings can create such a system?

Importance of these kingdoms

Humans did not create themselves; no one decided when they appeared on Earth or when they were to leave. Likewise, we do not determine the standards of success for human existence.

We are born into the same spiritual kingdom, the Kingdom of Darkness. At birth, we don't arrive with rules on how to live in this kingdom; we are taught and influenced to follow its dictates, norms, and values. When we reach the point of cognitive accountability, which means we understand well enough to make this type of decision, we <u>must</u> choose to remain as subjects to the Kingdom of Darkness or become citizens of the Kingdom of Light.

Until our bodies die, we all remain in the realm of the Kingdom of Darkness. Let me illustrate.

Born in the realm of the Kingdom of Darkness and remain as its citizen

Let's say you were born in Canada, so you're Canadian. You may visit the US and take part in its life, infrastructure, and culture. Though content to enjoy the beauty and whatever benefits it affords, you have no desire to live permanently in US nor to follow its laws and constitution. In this way, there's no need to change your citizenship. You already have default citizenship, so you'll maintain that until you pass on. You were born Canadian, you die Canadian. You did not decide to change that.

Born in the realm of the Kingdom of Darkness but choose to be a citizen of the Kingdom of Light

Using the same scenario where you're Canadian from birth. At some point, you learned about the US, and want to become more than a visitor. You want to assume the responsibility of a US Citizen and enjoy the benefits permanently.

CHAPTER 3: THE TWO KINGDOMS – STRUCTURE

Following the prescribed path, you became a US Citizen, renouncing your Canadian citizenship. You may continue to travel back and forth between the US and Canada. However, now that you're a US Citizen, you'll follow all the laws and regulations of the US, the new country (kingdom) you have chosen. You were born Canadian; you'll live and die American. You made a choice.

So it is when we choose to become a citizen of the Light. Until we die, our body remains within the influence of the Kingdom of Darkness, while our spirits are connected and are under the power and influence of the Kingdom of Light.

These two spiritual kingdoms are in this world – they make decisions, control, and influence people, and we are subject to their rule. **They are not voted on; they don't need our permission to exist. We influence and participate only to the extent we are aware of and are complicit in our interaction with these kingdoms.**

What we see happening worldwide is based on what these kingdoms allow, to meet their goals and objectives.

We experience these kingdoms by connecting ourselves to them via the intangible part of ourselves, the **spirit**. Everything we do starts from the spirit to the soul, then to our physical body.

As we follow the dictates of each kingdom, change begins from our spiritual connection, then transfers to the external physical realm. We first receive information within our thoughts and minds, which directs our actions.

Though **humans cohabit the same physical space on Earth, we are of different kingdoms, with opposing values and rules.** This results in tension, conflicts, and war. We add to this mess when **there is no clear, visible demarcation between the humans** of the Kingdom of Darkness and those in the Kingdom of Light. We treat everyone as if we are of the same Kingdom, and when we don't think, believe, or act like each other, we get irritated, angry, and even violent.

We incorrectly believe our conflict is within religion, politics, economic or social contracts; however, it goes far beyond these. **The conflicts between the Kingdoms are at a level and dimension far beyond the reach of human control.**

Learning about these Kingdoms will give us a picture or image of life that will help us interpret what we see and experience. It will also give us a tool to live freely and confidently irrespective of the changes or calamities that confront us.

"The Trouble with X"[9] and "The Emperor's New Clothes"

As we discuss a new framework, be aware of our human propensities. Hans Christian Andersen's classic story *"The Emperor's New Clothes"* is an illustration of how we might accept or reject the notion of The Two Kingdoms. If you're not familiar with this fairy tale, here's a summary from Wikipedia (2023):

"Two swindlers arrive at the capital city of an emperor who spends lavishly on clothing at the expense of state matters. Posing as weavers, they offer to supply him with magnificent clothes that are invisible to those who are stupid or incompetent. The emperor hires them, and they set up looms and go to work. A succession of officials, and then the emperor himself, visit them to check their progress. Each sees that the looms are empty but pretends otherwise to avoid being thought a fool.

Finally, the weavers report that the emperor's suit is finished. They mime dressing him, and he sets off in a procession before the whole city. The townsfolk uncomfortably go along with the pretense, not wanting to appear inept or stupid, until a child blurts out that the emperor is wearing nothing at all. The people then realize that everyone has been fooled. Although startled, the emperor continues the procession, walking more proudly than ever."[10]

"The Trouble with X" is a short essay by C.S Lewis that lays out the case we humans are incapable of seeing ourselves and others properly.

As in Andersen's story, and C.S Lewis' essay, we reject the clarity of the Two Kingdoms for several reasons, involving ignorance, arrogance, pride, and human desires:

Ignorance and arrogance

- Some are unaware of these kingdoms because they have not been taught or were misinformed.
- Some were taught, but like the emperor in the story, believe they are too intelligent to believe.

Pride and human desires

- Pride will cause us to think these are foolish notions and dismiss the whole idea of the spiritual realm.
- Pride will convince us we're inherently good and we are incapable of committing the atrocities we see others commit. We think the problems we face have nothing to do with us as individuals. After all, in every antagonistic encounter in history, we would have been the righteous ones, always making the right, perfect and moral decisions.
- We elevate our human desires above the truth. If the truth prevents us from fulfilling our human desires, we ignore the truth.
- We develop a third option of our own. Humans can be deceived into thinking we can create our own reality and, therefore, a third option. However, a third option is no option. **At the highest level, we have only Two Kingdoms.**

Chapter 4: The Two Kingdoms – Secrets

"But there is a God in heaven who reveals secrets."[11]

Do you wonder why we don't have spiritual conversations like this in the mainstream?

I grew up in church and have always accepted the concept of the intangible "spirit." The spirit may be thought of as a force that's inside us and around us that we interact with – without using the five senses. We've been taught to "Walk in the Spirit," and to obey the "Holy Spirit." We believed in the Trinity – Father, Son, and Holy Ghost. We've used terms like "good spirits" and "bad spirits." In the mainstream, we hear of gods, angels, demons, evil spirits, duppy, witchdoctors, the devil, obeah, voodoo, and the occult.

When I was young, growing up in a rural area, we had a neighbor who was demon-possessed. At night I would hear loud shrieks mixed with crying, screaming, and wailing. With trees between houses, her screaming words were incoherent, but I can still remember the feeling of fear and dread. What was happening over there sounded hellish and evil. The poor woman was tormented and terrorized.

Our district also had an obeahman with a thriving business, which I was told later was very lucrative and produced results. In later years, I was informed he was the most effective obeahman in our region. I think the connection is clear - **evil spirits have power.**

CHAPTER 4: THE TWO KINGDOMS – SECRETS

That sums up what I recall of spiritual things showing up in the physical realm. Until I went through the last few years of hellish experiences that forced me to reckon with reality. I found myself saying things I didn't believe and doing things I was against. At the moment of my error, I was convinced that what I was doing was right. But afterward, when I evaluated the facts, they didn't add up. Looking back, I was behaving in a way that didn't agree with my core beliefs. It was confusing, and I couldn't grasp what was happening – it felt like trying to walk on ice. I am still trying to understand the gap, and how I arrived there.

My conclusion is that the spiritual world is way more powerful than the physical, though we spend most of our lives relying on the physical. We interpret reality through our five senses. Sometimes we get a glimpse of the spiritual, but we seldom stop and investigate; we dismiss it as irrelevant. Because if everybody isn't talking about something, that thing doesn't exist, right? If our news reporters don't mention it, if it is not taught in schools, it doesn't exist, right?

Why is this not in the mainstream?

Speaking of spiritual matters can be scary. Even researching I was cautious about how far I went. I've heard enough of "don't play with Ouija boards because that thing works" to know to set boundaries for myself.

Black magic, the occult, and so on have been seen as the domain of a fringe group of people. The crazies, conspiracy theorists, those on the edge of society – nothing with which well-educated and sophisticated people would dabble. Though we might allow for the ultra-rich and famous to dabble in it as a means of entertainment.

Perhaps that's one of the reasons many stay clear of this domain. Some religions refer to an invisible deity but ignore the presence of opposing spirits. For example, our main monotheistic religions believe in an invisible God; however, they seldom teach on the opposing spirits to God.

In Christianity, we were told to "cast out demons," but that practice is all but ignored in modern churches, especially in the West.

When I hear of mass shootings, molestation of children, human trafficking, and other debasements of people – I know evil exists. Where evil exists, evil spirits are at work.

When addressing evil atrocities, we keep it at the surface level, punish the person or persons perpetuating that act, then move on. The pressure to accept whatever we're told keeps us in check. We have a restless feeling that we are missing something. It's a clue that there's more to us and the world. There's more than what we've been told or what we're allowed to see.

It helps Satan[12] if we remain ignorant of his work among us. He aims to convince people that there is no God. If that doesn't work, convince them that God exists, but Satan is fictitious. Humans could then attribute all that's good, bad, and indifferent to God, without credit to Satan.

But, if we could see we're living under Two Kingdoms, we would conclude that humans need to eliminate Satan and his minions, not God, nor other humans.

Chapter 5: The Two Kingdoms – Rule on Earth

What effect, if any, do these kingdoms have on us?

Let's start with a couple of questions:

- Do you believe you fully control every aspect of your life?
- How do you know the right things to do from birth until your body expires?
- What are the rules to live by to get what you want?
- What do you consider to be real?
- Who decides your parents, your siblings, and your children?
- Who decides where you were born? Continent? Country? State? Region?
- Who decides your ethnicity? Your height, eye color, skin color, hair color, and hair texture?
- Who decides if you are left-handed or right-handed?
- Who determines when you should appear on Earth? Who determines when you should depart?

Would you agree that many decisions were made **for you**, and without your consent? Are there other decisions you've made that are questionable whether **you** really made them?

- If and where you were educated or trained.
- The type of job or work you do.
- The communities that you are a part of.
- The kinds of pain and struggles you undergo.
- What you believe about yourself, about God or gods.

Let's consider the big systems and structures that we know are a part of:

Your Occupation and Work

How do you earn a living, what do you trade for money? Is it compatible and does it flow with what you sense as your purpose on earth? Does it provide meaning or is it just a means to an end?

Your Family and Community

How do you relate to people you were told are your relations? Could community be more important than we think? Who should decide how the community should be arranged and defined?

Your ability to live and move freely across the earth

We all arrive on earth as babies. Who determines that we must have permission to move to another area?

Why is it okay to pay an exorbitant sum of money for land, when land is a commodity not created by any human?

Your home, shelter, and housing

Who determines how the earth should be divided? How is it that we have so much uninhabited land, and **at the same time**, we have so many people with nowhere to live?

Your sustenance and food

CHAPTER 5: THE TWO KINGDOMS – RULE ON EARTH

We have an overabundance of food in some areas. Using technology in farming and packaging, we have food that can stay fresh for years. We have courier services zipping across the world, and we have transportation that can get almost anywhere within 24 hours. Why should anyone on Earth starve?

Your physical covering and clothing
What's the purpose of our clothes? Why the preoccupation with them?

Your wealth and money
What is money? What decides it should be critical for life? Who or what causes its scarcity?

Your health and wellbeing
The natural environment has lots of healing organisms and plants; plus, more and more doctors are graduating from college each year. Shouldn't the law of supply and demand cause healthcare to be available, accessible in abundance, and as affordable as food?

Does it feel like all these systems are well-controlled and well-organized, but you benefit less from them? What we're experiencing is real, and most of our worries and concerns are created within these major systems; systems governed by principalities, powers, and rulers of this world:

- Economics (Financial, Corporate)
- Education (Academia)
- Sports and Entertainment
- Farming and other food suppliers
- Government

- Information and technology
- Medical and pharmaceutical
- Religion
- Transportation

Who benefits? Who is in control of these systems? Who told you to give control of your lives to these entities? Who told you you'd "die" if you don't follow everyone else? Who told you your only option on earth is to comply with "society," allow yourself to be spoon-fed to distraction, and offer your body as a sacrifice for the benefit and pleasure of others?

Imagine a simplistic world, where you were part of a community that lived off the land, where members contribute according to their skills and abilities, and where you care for the other members as much as you care for yourself. Where plants and other natural resources are continually replenished as they are treated with care. Where knowledge was freely shared, where no one hoards anything, and you eat only until you're content. You consume everything only to the point of satisfaction and contentment, never hoarding. You live neither in scarcity nor excess. Where you travel and roam wherever you wish. Where there are no language or communication barriers. Where we have sufficient shelters, where we have no need for keys or padlocks. Where everyone has a place to sleep.

A community where you don't spend time competing and comparing with the other members. A community where there are no strangers.

Does this kind of life resonate with you? Would it add joy and peace to your soul?

The rulers of our communities and systems determine the rules that are allowed and enforced. Many are enforced in ways that are not visible. We accept them as "societal norms" or "societal expectations," "that's how it has always been," and "it's just common sense." We are also influenced, taught, and controlled by the information provided, by what is permitted in our environment, the laws that are passed, and the people who are appointed.

Satan is the ruler of this earth, working through these systems to oppress humans. God gave him power and authority **for now**. God still works among us through people, which explains the goodness that is still in the world. One day, this struggle and these massively corrupt systems will end.

That will be God's RESET.

So, what started this struggle?

Chapter 6: The Two Kingdoms – Declaration of War

"Too many of us are breaking down instead of breaking through" – CJ Johnson, 3/26/2022

Once there was one kingdom with God ruling Supreme along with His angels. Satan, described as beautiful, was one of God's higher-ranking angels who had access to God's inner circle[13].

Before we humans arrived on earth, God ensured everything was in place to sustain us. Earth's location, conditions, and placement were made perfect for human. Scientists call where Earth is situated the Goldilocks zone – Earth is "the only astronomical object known to harbor life." To create a perfectly suited zone, our Creator must have had perfect knowledge of us, at the molecular level.

God has a plan to extend His family to include humans who live, interact, and rule like Him. When He placed us in this idyllic environment, he gave us the job of a caretaker and assigned us a position that was a little lower than angels. He planned to teach us to live as fully human, with a spirit that connects with Him. At first, we didn't need laws, but our relationship progressed organically as we walked and talked with Him like parents and children. We were contented and fulfilled, in harmony with each other and our environment. The animals weren't wild, the environment wasn't harsh, and we didn't need to find food,

CHAPTER 6: THE TWO KINGDOMS – DECLARATION OF WAR

clothing, or shelter.

Then the ruler of the Kingdom of Darkness stepped in and deceived us by tricking us into obeying him. When we obey Satan, we disconnect from God. Whom we obey becomes our master, so by obeying Satan, we have chosen him as our master. By disconnecting from God, we are disconnected from life. We've lost life physically, with decaying bodies. But more importantly, we became spiritually dead. From then until now, there has not been peace on earth, nor will there be, while Satan rules.

Though physically we remained alive, everything started to die. Animals have become wild and dangerous, making everything in the environment difficult and decaying. Satan's spirits create havoc and mayhem, disunity, hate, and rage.

We've had to work hard to find food, clothing, and shelter. Our relationships are tumultuous, while some are life-giving, others involve hate, gossip, anger, envy, malice, and other spirit-crushing shenanigans.

Satan is the ruler of Earth's domain; every human born on Earth is automatically in his kingdom. Our allegiance remains with the Kingdom of Darkness, and the only way to leave is by (spiritual) death - renouncing Satan and accepting the Kingdom of Light.

Today the world is nowhere near its original beauty; each successive generation has attempted to fix it – to live happily with no pain or suffering. Each has failed, but they've created new challenges with every failure. It feels like the current generations have figured we have exhausted all human options, and now they are giving up – checking out.

Meanwhile, a feeling of unease continues at our level. Some folks are leaning in to understand, some are praying for divine intervention, others are refusing to participate, and others are charging ahead to snip off anything they perceive as a threat. Others have recoiled for personal protection and control, and others are on the warpath to challenge and cut off anyone, and anything they believe has caused this malady.

While humans frantically continue this war, the spiritual rulers continue to build and execute plans put in place from the beginning of our time.

So, what happened at the beginning?

Chapter 7: The Two Kingdoms – History

The two kingdoms started when Satan challenged God and was tossed to earth, along with a group of followers (fallen angels). They are the rulers of this earth, with gods appointed over nations and regions. However, God remains Sovereign; God of all gods, Lord of all lords, King of all kings. Though Satan was an angel, he was still a created being, a servant to God, while humans were created to be children of God. As His children, we were created to be like Him.

What else I've learned about Satan:

- Satan and other angels would periodically present themselves before God and chat about what was going on earth.
- Other angels were placed on earth to watch over us. However, they were captivated by the beautiful earth women whom they married and had children. The offspring of these angels and human women were giants.
- Humankind was threatened by this transhuman lawlessness and depravity, which angered God and led to His intervention with the Great Flood[14].

When Satan was expelled and set up his kingdom on earth, this created the second kingdom. When he left heaven, Satan took one-third of the angels with him. And when you add the fallen angels who were set to watch over humans, who later disobeyed, along with the spirits of the giants – real giants – Satan has a large army at his disposal.

Nonetheless, there are more angels in God's army. If the numbers weren't encouraging enough, Satan is nowhere as powerful as God. Satan's power is only comparable to that of a powerful angel.

Throughout human history, Satan has been trying to corrupt humans:

- He deceived the first humans (Adam and Eve) into obeying him, causing them to sin, and to lose their position as God's children.
- Through the angels who were watchers, he corrupted the human genes with sexual relations with women. The offspring were an aberration, not fit to be called God's children, and not fit to defeat Satan.
- Through Pharaoh, he attempted genocide of God's chosen people while they were slaves in Egypt.
- Through Haman, he attempted genocide of God's chosen people during King Xerxes' reign.
- Through Herod, he killed all the young male toddlers in an attempt to kill Jesus.
- Through Nero, he attempted genocide of Jesus' followers.
- Through the Crusaders, he attempted to tarnish God's Good News to the world.
- Through Hitler, he attempted genocide of God's chosen people.
- Through the latest anti-Christ, he attempts to use science and technology to wipe out humans and redefine humanity.
- Through the current corrupt systems, he is trying to get humans distracted, overworked, and confused, and thus they focus on the physical. They fail to understand their value and purpose to live fulfilling, joyful lives starting **now**.

CHAPTER 7: THE TWO KINGDOMS – HISTORY

If Satan can convince us that all pain and suffering has nothing to do with him, then we can continue in denial and never seek the real solution. The solution is <u>death</u>, but not ANY death. A human death, but not ANY <u>human</u>. It must be the <u>perfect</u> human. And there is only one perfect human!

We must die spiritually to Satan to be released from Satan's clutches. Throughout the ages, he has convinced us to offer sacrifice to him – and many have sacrificed loved ones, even children, to him. However, that was and continues to be a fraudulent exchange. Sacrificing to Satan brings physical and spiritual death.

Satan is a fraud, a scammer. He sounds like the real deal, but he is not. Here is what the real deal is like.

God created a perfect sacrifice, Himself, in human form as Jesus Christ. His physical body died; however, His power is unlimited. He was able to raise Himself from the dead. As God, He did not experience spiritual death and could return with a new body. He ascended and is alive in that new body.

Satan, sin, death, and hell have no control over Him.

That's what we are prevented from knowing: humans get to follow Christ along the same path – die, then rise to life. To access this road, we need to know the truth:

1. The perfect God knows everything about us - our mistakes, wretched thoughts, and missteps, also known as Sin. The payment for Sin is death. Even before Christ arrived on Earth, in Exodus 34:6-7 God describes Himself as *" Yahweh! The Lord! The God of* **compassion** *and* **mercy**! *I am* ***slow to anger*** *and filled with* **unfailing love** *and* **faithfulness**..." The tension that we sometimes fail to grasp is that God loves us unconditionally, yet our sin separates us from Him.
2. Before we die physically, we can bridge the gap and pay for our

Sin. **Only Christ can bridge the gap and make the payment.** We can't work to pay our way.
3. We need only to turn to Jesus Christ and accept Him as Savior. He guarantees that He'll not turn anyone away who approaches Him with sincerity.
4. After we die, He'll either welcome us home or send us away from His presence.

Satan tries hard to fool us. We should know the real deal, or we will be deceived - offering him all our worldly and spiritual possessions, thinking he can deliver. When we work excessively on acquiring what we think we need, we don't have enough time to learn to live properly. We live reactively and are off-balance.

Satan continues to ask us to sacrifice to him to get what we want. We have complied with blood sacrifice in wars, murders, abortion, mass shootings, and genocide. We have complied with skepticism, disbelief, man-made rituals, offerings, and religious paths that get us to one of his gods or nowhere.

Chapter 8: The Plan – Kingdom of Light

"All the people of the earth
are nothing compared to Him.
He does as He pleases
among the angels of heaven
and among the people of the earth.
No one can stop Him or say to Him,
'What do you mean by doing these things?'"[15]

I get it when I hear someone say that God is all-powerful and could have ruled differently, He could have chosen another way. I get it: my kids say the same kind of thing to me. They question my intellect and love – how is it we have ice cream, I could make ANY decision, yet I refuse to give them ice cream for dinner? That makes no sense!

But we are not God, His thoughts and ways are far beyond me[16]. But I am convinced, if I knew what He knows, I would do exactly what He is doing. I was reminded of Marvel's movie The Avengers: Infinity War:

Thanos needed the full set of infinity stones to be all-powerful. Dr. Strange was the guardian of the time stone so, in effect, he could evade Thanos indefinitely. Despite his pledge to guard the stone with his life, Dr. Strange gave up the infinity stone, presumably to save Tony Stark's life. It seemed like a bad trade to exchange the world for one man. When Stark asked Dr. Strange why he did that, Dr. Strange simply said, "We're in the end game now."

The world was in chaos and fear, the Avengers were being wiped out, and there was no possible option for the Avengers to win against Thanos.

In the follow-on movie, EndGame, Dr. Strange explained that he gave up the stone because he went through billions of possible futures, and only one yielded a victorious outcome for the Avengers. That option required him to give up the stone.

In the end, this seemingly illogical decision by Dr. Strange was the perfect solution to save the world.

At first, it appeared Dr. Strange traded the world for Stark. In the end, Stark's death was the key to saving the world. **Only with perfect information can we see the best and only solution to save the world.**

God's plan from the beginning was to have a big ol' family of humans. As His children, we would resemble Him, living freely and creatively, where there's no need for policing or enforcement.

This ideal world would be where His family would live forever, experiencing His love and loving one another. They would lack nothing and be in harmony with each other, the environment, and everything within the universe. We would all be original, with different fingerprints, DNA, and personalities. We'd never be bored.

Today, **this is still the plan**. There isn't much for humans to do, our burden is light. It is God who is doing the heavy lifting. God's operations appear to include:

1. Helping humans know who they are and to embrace their identity.
2. Helping humans believe, trust, and desire His kingdom.
3. Helping humans know their history, present, and future.
4. Extracting humans from Satan's control, that is - rid humans of

CHAPTER 8: THE PLAN – KINGDOM OF LIGHT

   sin and death.
5. Restraining Satan, his demons, and evil spirits – forever.
6. Creating a new heaven and earth for those who join His family.
7. Placing the humans who have chosen Him and His kingdom, on this new earth, and live among them.
8. Being in an intimate love relationship with humans, as a good Father.

God knows, on our own, we're no match for Satan, plus we easily succumb to our desires.

Satan and other spirits do not have a physical body, they are therefore not as susceptible to doing wrong. That's not the same with humans. Humans have a physical body, which provides more opportunities for failure. It's no wonder we are referred to as sheep.

When we meet our human desires illegitimately, we produce sin, which leads to all kinds of death. God's plan is to eradicate all these – sins, death, Satan, and his angels.

Not only is God working through His plan to crush Satan, but He's also working on getting humans to an idyllic existence. To get there, we must want to be with Him, willingly. In this physical body, we have one major decision to make – to choose Him or not.

If you're like me, you might have a couple more questions here: if God could get rid of Satan right *then, why didn't he?* Also, as God, He would have known Satan would be appointed ruler of the earth, why create him? For an answer, I considered the account of Job in the Bible.

The incident went like this:

It began with Satan visiting God along with other angels. God bragged about a human, Job, who was faithful to Him. Satan countered that Job's faithfulness was only because God gave him (Job) riches, wealth, and fame. God disagreed, and to prove His point, He allowed Satan to wreak havoc on Job – Satan killed Job's children and livestock and destroyed everything he owned. Later even sores broke out on Job's body. But Satan was not allowed to take Job's life or wife. In the end, Job never turned away from God and received twice the number of livestock and other property, except children. [He received one new set of children; though the first set died physically, they were still alive spiritually].

With a story like that in a whole book in the Bible, I'm left with these thoughts:

1. I am baffled that we don't speak more candidly about spiritual matters involving both God and Satan.
2. God is not an impersonal, inflexible dictator. He communicates and is open to raw, authentic conversations with us.
3. I don't think and reason like God. (Seriously, He gave permission for Satan to mess with us!)
4. It's not everything humans consider "good" or "successful" is from God, and not everything we consider "bad" or, "failure" is of the devil. We can evaluate these accurately only from God's perspective.

These are my takeaways:

- Initially, human beings were meant to live forever.
- Once humans chose to live under Satan's rule, they started to die. No human will live forever on earth while under Satan's kingdom.
- Human beings are also spirits; our spirit lives on even after the physical body dies.
- With permission, Satan can destroy our physical bodies, but only God can kill the spirit. Also, only God can create spirits by breathing life into people.
- We are not to fear any human or Satan. We are to fear only God.

CHAPTER 8: THE PLAN – KINGDOM OF LIGHT

To truly live, **we need help**, and real help must be greater and more powerful than Satan's.

Chapter 9: The Plan – Kingdom of Darkness

While God provided a handbook outlining His plan for us to understand and follow, Satan isn't that transparent. We have had to gauge Satan's plans by what God says about him, and the supporting evidence Satan provides us throughout history.

The war is between Satan and God. They are fighting for human souls. Satan wants humans to worship him. He doesn't care whether human bodies live or die as long as their spirits don't follow God.

Satan has won many battles; however, we seldom recognize him as the victor. By convincing us he had no part in these "victories," Satan reaps the added benefit of some thinking God doesn't care, is incompetent, or at least, non-existent.

We might see the prevalence of satanic churches and believe those are benign, just another religion. We might believe that's the extent of Satan's influence. But his influence is **greater**, much greater. From the beginning, Satan has had his hands in every area of influence, including the church. It is said that the best lie has a grain of truth. Many religions, churches, and denominations have been created and sustained by Satan. In some cases, there's a subtle difference between the real or authentic and those that are not. It is easy to miss the difference, and even ardent Christians are deceived. It is easier to spot religions that practice rituals or ideologies, which we may label "cultish" or "weird;" however, many

CHAPTER 9: THE PLAN – KINGDOM OF DARKNESS

that appear "normal" are deep-seated deceptions as they are seen as acceptable and mainstream, especially when they have many followers.

Humans' time on earth is fleeting compared to Satan's life span. Time is dismissive to Satan as he is playing the long game; while humans are trying to hoard, spend, and do all we can within an average 70 years. Seventy years are nothing to Satan. Even those of us who believe that our spirit lives forever, **live as though we value the average 70-odd years more than the infinity that follows.**

With many wanting to fill the ego with power, pleasure, and prestige, Satan is not short of people to convince.

As the Father of Lies, Satan preys on human desires and proclivities, so he presents himself as the fulfillment of our earthly desires. He'll meet those desires in exchange for obedience. And humans gladly comply, especially if we were asking the same from God, which God has denied. He attacks from many fronts and bombards our minds with accusations and lies. He distracts us and stirs trouble among us.

You might ask, so what's wrong with that? Each person living their own life? Following Satan or our desires, living the life we have, choosing to live this life as if it is the only one?

Good question.

It's like a reflex for those who know what's really going on. It's the kind of question you'd ask someone who runs into a burning building to save someone asleep inside. You see the fire; you know what will happen if you don't act.

As humans, we were made as caretakers; if we've lost that, it means Lucifer is succeeding in ridding us of our humanity. Granted, we are not to force, harass or intimidate others to believe anything. We should respect and agree that each one's decision is their own responsibility.

And that's how it will be in the end. **Everyone will be respected for their decision, and they'll get what they've asked for. None of us is good enough to live with a perfect God, we all sin, so we all need a**

Savior.

In the meantime, we live in a symbiotic relationship with other humans. We're trying to understand ourselves, our world, and others. We mess up, they mess up, we get into trouble, and we cause trouble. We don't know when our time is up. But **we must decide before our time is up.** Otherwise, we'll live a life without God. *I don't know what that's like, but I imagine it would be living with my greatest fears, experiencing all the pain I've caused and experienced – all happening at the same time. All the time. With no hope for it to end. At least, in this life, no matter what we undergo, we know there will be an end, with our physical death.*

If that weren't enough, Satan and his gods and spirits are constantly pummeling us with real-life challenges – remember those systems mentioned earlier. He thwarts our attempt to get to the Truth. When we learn the Truth, or at least get close, that doesn't deter him. He has many tricks. He'll even create diversions for his diversions. We cannot outsmart the devil on our own.

He has members and helpers everywhere. He is so clever: he has even convinced us that we can have allegiance to him and God simultaneously. But have you ever seen darkness and light coexisting in a single space? **You'll see darkness only if there's no light.** Once light shows up, darkness disappears.

So, it is, the prevalence of darkness in our world isn't because Satan is stronger than God. It is because 1) God has given him powers, and 2) we Christians have been retreating and hiding our light.

Chapter 10: The Plan – Human Efforts

"As they plot their crimes, they say, "We have devised the perfect plan!" Yes, the human heart and mind are cunning."..."No human wisdom or understanding or plan can stand against the Lord."[17]

Often, I've heard we are in control of our destiny, we are gods and can solve our own problems. There is some truth to this mindset; however, it is incomplete. We have some control and ability to solve some of our problems, but many decisions are made that are outside of our ability and control. We need to understand our place within the decision-making hierarchy.

As he did initially, the devil continues to promise people what they already have. He promised Eve she would be like God, knowing good from evil. Adam and Eve were already created in the likeness and image of God, they didn't need to know good and evil to live like God. Today, we are making the same decision as our original parents, to **pursue knowledge and live trying to be our own gods**. We work hard to provide for our needs; we search and research ways to protect, guide, and be independent and self-sufficient as our own god. When we fail, we restart the process, seldom questioning our original broken hypothesis that we are gods.

Acquire Knowledge

Satan and his cronies have been helping humans, sharing information and skills that weren't supposed to be shared with humans.

He doesn't openly take credit, so people might believe we humans are more impressive than we really are. As a result, we look to ourselves and misappropriate these accomplishments, thereby ignoring God and Satan. Today we are perplexed that despite our stunning "human" advancement, we cannot eradicate basic social ills. We've missed the point. **Humans and anything made by humans cannot save humans.**

The devil is on earth to build his physical kingdom and will trade with us to get what he wants. God, the Creator of humans, knows our greatest need is of a spiritual nature. He knows we cannot heal ourselves, so He came and fixed our spiritual dilemma. '**The fix is in**', but many still don't know because the devil has us running around trying to fix physical problems.

Abraham Maslow was a psychologist known for his work, Maslow's Hierarchy of Needs, depicted:

CHAPTER 10: THE PLAN – HUMAN EFFORTS

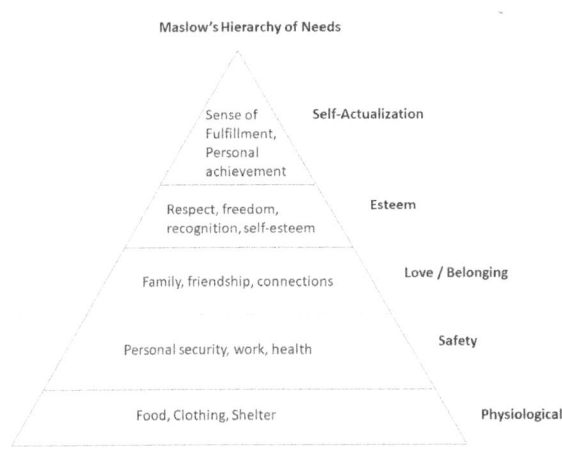

Abraham Maslow's Hierarchy of Needs

Using the shape of a pyramid, starting at the base, he depicts the priority of how humans meet their needs from the basic physiological need for food, shelter, and clothing to self-actualization. As the need at each level is met, we strive to meet the need of the next higher level, and so on until we get to the ideal level of self-actualization.

Whether or not we are aware of Maslow's theory, many of us follow this principle. Starting at the base of the pyramid, we meet our needs within each level, prioritizing the upper levels only after the lower levels are satisfied. Adults spend their entire lives working hard to provide food, clothing, and shelter. Many don't go beyond meeting their basic needs and therefore might not feel a sense of satisfaction and fulfillment.

Think of what might happen if you'd ask a person who was hungry to participate in an activity that takes them away from getting food. They might say, "I can't think of that now, I need to eat first, and then I can think of that." Their entire attention would be focused on finding food.

Depending on our belief systems and society, we may depend on ourselves, governments, or others to supply these needs.

The I AM (Inverted Abraham Maslow) Hierarchy of Needs

Still, there are others who don't follow Maslow's hierarchy. Though they might not have enough food or sufficient shelter, they've reached a level of contentment beyond the financially wealthy. Studies have shown that people on the African Continent, though lacking the physical wealth associated with Western Countries, are some of the happiest. Their level of happiness points to their commitment to human dignity, community, and spiritual resilience.

I've used Maslow's hierarchy and found it lacking. I've found that it needs two major changes:

1. **Flip it upside-down.** Meeting our need for self-actualization should begin earlier. We don't need to acquire stuff before we get to the correct sense of self. Knowing and appreciating ourselves sets the foundation to acquire the right trappings. Plus, the whole journey will be more fun!
2. **Start with the spiritual.** The path to a fulfilling life doesn't start with physical needs, but spiritual. It continues to be sustained by the spiritual. When our work to meet physical needs is fueled by the **spiritual,** the result is more fulfilling and requires less physical stress.

CHAPTER 10: THE PLAN – HUMAN EFFORTS

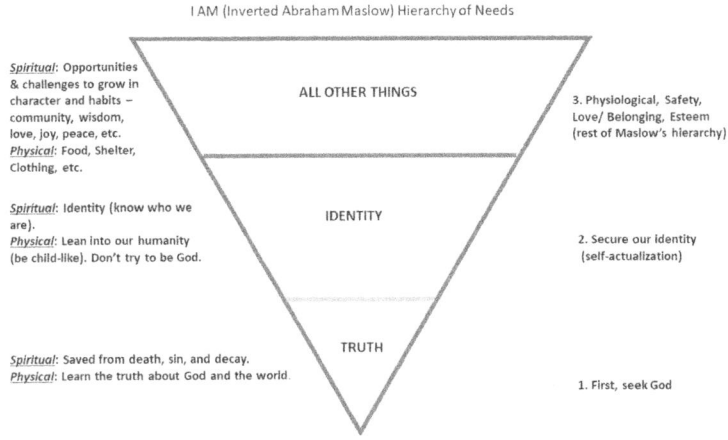

I AM (Inverted Abraham Maslow) Hierarchy of Needs

When we flip Maslow's pyramid and start with Truth and Identity, we'll encounter God. If we make this optimal decision to start with Truth and choose to live in the Kingdom of Light, we are set for success. The next need is to know ourselves and start to live as citizens of the Kingdom of Light. This is where self-actualization starts. And if what we believe about God and ourselves is the truth, we'll have confidence and the ability to tackle life. When we try to get navigate life while confused about the world, we're doomed to disappointment, heartache, and pain – for ourselves and others.

Unfortunately, many of us learn about ourselves only after becoming adults. This is a cautionary tale to me as a parent. My priority is to tell my children the truth while validating their reality. The process of self-actualization happens now. As humans, they should know to embrace conflicts and challenges as opportunities to become whole. To be anchored in their identity, accepting they will never be perfect, and at the same time, knowing they're loved beyond their imagination. Any wealth, food, and shelter they acquire would be in accordance with their character – so they'll always have enough. Not so much that they forget God and not so little they'll start thinking He doesn't care. And living joyfully in the tension between too much and too little. Recreation would be to uplift their spirits along with others and never to the debasement or demise of anyone.

This hierarchy prevents the damaging effect of imposing self-actualization based on what is not Truth. That kind of self-actualization produces pride, arrogance, boredom, and a sense of entitlement.

Human advancements

Satan's focus on our physical advancement has nothing to do with helping humans. It's to help the Kingdom of Darkness advance its devilish plans.

But we feel pride in our fantastic knowledge, even though we still lack wisdom and truth. *To someone without wisdom and truth, giving them information is like giving someone fire without guidance on how to use it. A wise person will place fire in the fireplace; an unwise person will misuse the fire, perhaps even placing it on their nice warm sofa.*

Though the devil is clever and cunning, he lacks wisdom and truth. Let's take, for example, our knowledge of controlling the weather. We have been doing this for years, yet when did you last hear us discuss our manipulation's impact on global weather change? Couldn't places like Malawi on the African continent, which depend on farming but receive little rainfall, benefit from this technology?

Resources are allocated based on the dictates of the Kingdom of Darkness and not based on human needs. So, you'll understand why it's perplexing to ordinary people why decisions are made that are of little to no benefit to hurting humans.

Live forever

Satan appeals to our god complex by promising us what we already have – the ability to live forever. We desire to live forever because we were made to live forever. There's a rumor circulating that the current generation will be the last as we have biotechnology to sustain this generation forever. But this is not new information. Every generation lives forever; it's only a question of where.

I imagine some of us are excited by the prospect of prolonging this earthly experience. Others may desire this ability to prove they are God, and no higher God exists. Some may see this as human being's final triumph over death. And because of human ingenuity and skills, we've found a way to live forever. We trust biotechnology to fulfill our desire to rid our human body of all limitations. To create our own heaven on earth.

The rumor would be closer to the truth if said: "The current generation will be the last generation that lives upon the current earth." Whether the current generation will be the last to arrive on this earth, I don't know, but there will be a last generation on this earth, as the earth we live on will not last forever. This is not to say we should abuse the earth, but that we should not worship it, but care for it and hug it loosely.

Have full control

Leaders might vocalize that they're free and independent, sometimes espousing what they will do and accomplish[18]. This mindset may project confidence to the masses and encourage people to give up their individual rights and allow others to take responsibility. However, the Two Kingdoms dictate what our leaders can or can't do.

It appears world leaders are planning to rely on scientific knowledge and technology to dictate:

- How we live a happy life on earth.
- How we organize for a sustainable future, using mind and physical

control.
- How to direct people's actions to care for the physical earth, especially as we haven't identified an alternate planet to sustain human life.
- How to live forever and be our own gods, or at least, without God.

Earlier civilizations may have tried to accomplish these goals, but since they no longer exist, it is safe to assume they failed.

We have compelling evidence of powerful, skillful, and knowledgeable civilizations that existed on Earth before our recorded history. I believe it's arrogant to assume we as individuals are more advanced than they were. We might be impressed by the tools we have created, but inside, we are still a sinful bunch heading for death; with only one solution to be saved.

Humanity has a sin problem in our spirits and a death problem in our bodies. We ignore the spirit problem and will try to eradicate the word "sin" as it triggers the Kingdom of Darkness. Science and technology will not save humanity, as they focus only on the body, making it an incomplete solution. Being entertained and stimulated to oblivion provides no meaningful benefit to the human soul.

The Ultimate Human Being

Our goal is to become the ultimate human being. As we build technologies to create the ultimate human being, we might miss the obvious; we already have a tried-and-true standard to model, **Jesus Christ.** He lived on this physical earth. He experienced all the hardships of life that we do. Yet He conquered all the constraints and challenges of this physical earth – sin (hardship) and death, and He's alive today and forever.

The people who lived with Him more than 2000 years ago started to tell everyone about Him while He was still here. Before these people

CHAPTER 10: THE PLAN – HUMAN EFFORTS

died, they wrote down their experiences. Their account created the last 27 books of the Bible, known as the New Testament.

From their account, this is their portrait of Him:

- He lacks nothing. He creates anything He wants whenever He wants, without technology.
- He controls nature.
- He cannot be contaminated. When He touches disease, the disease dies, not Him.
- He raised Himself and others from the dead; death has no power over Him.
- Time and space are of no limitation to Him.
- He is more powerful than His worst enemy.
- Real people gravitated toward Him. He feeds them with words that give life, healing, and restoration.
- He is most powerful and uses that power to love.
- He is alive today and will physically return to take sole control of our world government.

Is that what we want too? We're using technology as a stepping stone to reach the perfect human body. Granted, Jesus is God in human form. He's also the Son of God, which makes His followers, adopted brothers and sisters.

As His adopted siblings, His followers also share the family's characteristics.

Eventually, we'll all get a body that lasts forever, but it won't be via technology or tools built by human hands. We are too corrupt to create anything pure. Let's not allow the devil to convince us to join him in getting a forever body when we are already guaranteed one.

So, God and Satan each have a plan, and humans are divided between the two. The Kingdoms have their own agenda, fighting over the souls of humans. Everyone knows what's at stake except unsuspecting humans. They are getting hurt and killed, seeing the carnage, and experiencing battle fatigue. But they can't understand why.

Let's take a closer look at this war...

Chapter 11: The War Operation

The plan that humans have is not their plan, but they're being made to believe it's their plan. The strategies will be based on what's happening within the spiritual kingdoms; Earth's terrain is only the battlefield.

> "Why are the nations so angry?
> Why do they waste their time with futile plans?
> The kings of the earth prepare for battle;
> the rulers plot together against the Lord
> and against His anointed one.
> "Let us break their chains," they cry,
> "and free ourselves from slavery to God."
> But the One who rules in heaven laughs.
> The Lord scoffs at them.
> Then in anger, He rebukes them,
> terrifying them with His fierce fury.
> For the Lord declares, "I have placed my chosen king on the throne
> in Jerusalem, on My holy mountain."[19]

God's strategy is known only to Him and to whomever He chooses to communicate. Though He provided us with a Book documenting His intentions and instructions, He must decode it for the reader. He reveals the truth to some and keeps it hidden from others.

For example, at Jesus' birth, three wise men from the East traveled to see the birth of the King of the world, yet political and religious elites had no idea that the baby arrived in their own town.

See the Appendix for more details on the war. It outlines some of God's operations[20] alongside Satan's guerilla warfare:

War operations from the enemy's camp

Lucifer doesn't present himself as the enemy of humans. It's quite the opposite: he presents himself as an angel of light, helpful to human beings. He gives humans what they desire, and what we desire is usually based on our selfish preoccupation and passions. With our ignorance and ego, when we get what we want, we assume the benefactor must be good and right.

He knows human beings better than humans know themselves, and with that advantage, he has successfully manipulated and deceived us in many ways:

Covertly

- Works through the gods of this world to create systems that manipulate and enslave humans.
- Presents images of himself as a silly, laughable character, wearing a red suit and carrying a pitchfork in books, movies, and other areas of popular culture.
- Establishes and promotes religions that are close, some very close, to the Truth, but not quite.
- He knows there's one way to salvation, so he has presented innumerable compelling alternatives to humans to entice them from that One Way.
- Mocks and belittles the One Way. He appeals to the human ego to consider a single solution to be ludicrous and backward.

CHAPTER 11: THE WAR OPERATION

- Infiltrates Christ's churches, creating confusion and disunity.
- Creates divisions and disunity among people. If people were to be united, we could collate what we know as individuals, then create a mosaic that would reveal the Truth. The Truth would set us free from his dominion.

Overtly

- Establish Satanic churches, clubs, and other institutions.
- Promotes atheism and multiple other religions.
- Hijacks humans from knowing the Truth.
- Some are taught there are many ways to get to the Truth.
- Some of us are told fictional stories of how we fit into God's plan.
- Some are told God has no interest in what's going on in our lives.
- Some are told God sets this world in motion, then ignores it, and the life we have now is the only life we'll get, and we have no say in what comes after our body dies.
- Some are told the identity of the Intelligent Mind that created us. However, they are given faulty information or outright lies about how to connect with Him.
- Some receive instructions for connecting with God; however, the instructions divert the worship to other gods. *For them, it's like purchasing a plane ticket to travel to Australia but receiving a ticket to China. The ticket looks legitimate, but the instructions take you elsewhere. For others, it's like kids being kidnapped. The individual pretends to be trustworthy, showing the kid something that appeals to them – a cute toy or candy. Scammers are real.*
- Some call on spirits to empower them. Some of those spirits are real and have answered prayers. This is not proof that they are praying to the God of gods.[21] Satan can disguise himself as the angel of

light; he and his angels have supernatural powers and abilities.
- *If the spirit does not confess allegiance to Jesus Christ as Lord, they are from the Kingdom of Darkness.*

People may believe all real spirits are from God (Kingdom of Light). That is not so:

- We must differentiate the spirits. They are either from the Kingdom of Light or the Kingdom of Darkness.
- There is only one option or way to enter the Kingdom of Light (Heaven). There are infinite options for staying in the Kingdom of Darkness (Hell).

Chapter 12: Human Systems and Operations

"What are mere mortals that You should think about them, human beings that You should care for them?" [22]

The Kingdom of Darkness controls the current way of living on Earth, as Lucifer is the god of this world[23].

There are 168 hours per week. Out of this, we are expected to spend on average 40 hours working, plus additional hours to prepare for the work, travel and unwind from said work. Also, we need time to meet the obligations of our family and community and take care of ourselves and our loved ones. Plus, we need to sleep. As adults, we're expected to repeat this every year, year after year, except for a few weeks off.

For many, to make any major purchase, you must secure a loan, which means you cannot take a break from "adulting," because you have loans to pay off. The more you owe, the more commitments you make, and the more anxious and distressed you become. This continues until retirement. Depending on the job type, you won't have enough funds to stop working (retire), so you will keep at it until you drop dead. Work is good and healthy but the way we've organized our lives has corrupted the creativity and beauty of work.

More people are seeing the insanity of this and are demanding a change. The younger generation sees through the insanity and says, "Meh, no thanks!" I understand. I cringe when I remember how I used to live and defend this madness.

Our spirits are aligned with how we were created; we were never meant for an unimaginative, slavish, rote existence. Playing mindless video games and taking drugs as a full-time vocation is hellish to the soul!

We are heading forward to an ideal world. A world that'll involve the participation and cooperation of humans but won't be engineered or controlled by humans and Lucifer. We long to experience peace and joy. We want enough provisions not to worry about tomorrow and be able to spend time in leisure and meaningful work. We want to live without evil, without sickness and disease, in harmony with everyone, and never be fearful of the future or guilt-ridden by our past.

Various media and communities have expressed and observed a macro-level unease, a general disquiet in our spirits, a dissatisfaction with the status quo, and an expectation of something **revolutionary**.

In 2022, I heard Russell Brand in one of his podcasts short, "Who could save us?":

"I am trying to think of the people we would need to save us right now. I'm gonna put Churchill...Gandhi...St. Bernadette... St. Teresa...Julian of Norwich. You need people who understand the sacred, because the material world and our current systems are faltering and failing. We need a new kind of spiritual genius, but everything is being desacralized, everything is being banalised, everything is being turned into a kind of meaningless morass so that the one imperative to commodify and consume can be relentlessly pursued. Remember when we were obsessed with Islamism and Islamist terrorism, we talked about a fundamentalism, but their fundamentalism is no different from the fundamentalism under which you already live - Fundamentalist Materialism. If it can't be measured, if it can't be bought and sold, it doesn't

CHAPTER 12: HUMAN SYSTEMS AND OPERATIONS

have any meaning"[24].

I was amazed at his depth of perception. At that time I didn't know he had a deep spiritual outlook on life.

The world is in a mess because the ruler of the earth is actively working to keep it that way. We might blame people and institutions, believing they are the problem, but that's the ingenuity of Satan. The problem isn't merely people. It goes higher up.

Satan works through people, so when a mass murderer enters a school, we investigate the shooter. When they kidnap and traffic young people, we look at the smugglers. The shooter and smuggler appear to be working autonomously. When they are caught, we tend to ask why and try to find physical or psychological evidence to explain why they acted that way. Even with a manifesto, they might have an explanation, **but they really don't know**.

Those who devise our economic system may believe they are clever for doing so; they live with an air of invincibility because they think they've created a system that keeps them in power and financial security in perpetuity. A few people have more wealth than they can spend. And yet we have others who, despite their best efforts, can barely eke out a living. This might sound like capitalism but think again – it's **every** economic system. Wealth always flows toward the few, and away from the masses. This doesn't feel right, look right, or smell right, and that's because it's not right or godly. The devil does not discriminate; he is in every earthly system. He might use capitalism in one region, and communism in another.

I was born in Jamaica in the 1970s, so I had a taste of socialism. The taste of scarcity, insecurity, and fear still lingers with me. I remember going to shop for basic food items and having to "trust" (credit) because there was not enough money. And when we could buy, the items were scarce. So, in order to buy, say bread, it was "married" to a non-essential item, forcing us to buy what we didn't want to get what we need. The government and critical-thinking people were on opposing sides. Though, those in charge spoke with eloquence about how they really cared for poor people, the poor remained in poverty.

That was my personal experience with socialism, but if today you'd prefer to live in North Korea, and not South Korea; to live in Venezuela and not Brazil; raise your family in Haiti and not the Dominican Republic – I could see the appeal for communism. However, from a Kingdom perspective, Communism and Marxism must curtail the religion and freedom of the population. The Kingdom of Light requires us to have free will, as we are judged based on our free choice. Therefore, Communism and Marxism are not compatible with the Kingdom of Light, which means these systems are of Darkness.

God demonstrated His ideal government with the nation of ancient Israel – He ruled. God was the head of the nation until the people rejected Him and demanded a king, to be like other nations. God warned them that a king would send their children to war, enslave them, collect taxes from them, and use them as he wishes. The people insisted – they wanted a king they could see. So, they got a king. And, as you'd say, the rest is history. **We won't have any ideal systems until all humans reinstate God as the King of all.**

Satan's plans succeed by staying in the background. We're unaware that he exists, or the full extent of his involvement in our affairs. God has an arrest warrant for Satan and his accomplices, and it is being served. The battle takes place in our "neighborhood," and we're caught up in the exchange. It is not pretty.

We have citizens flooding the streets protesting injustices. We change governments, jobs, communities, relationships, or countries, but the problems persist. We seek solutions in science and technology, and

CHAPTER 12: HUMAN SYSTEMS AND OPERATIONS

we'll reap some positive results, but they are short-lived. History bears this out. Mankind on earth has never sustained advances made. We are prone to self-destruct. How would you explain the major civilizations that dominated the world and are gone or eclipsed by others? We are left with monuments like the Sphinx, pyramids, and other works of wonder. We see the monuments, but do we know what became of the civilizations that built them? What **really** happened to them?

If we knew that Satan was actively cajoling us, and his promptings made us deceive, complain, and succumb to depraved immorality, we might not give in so easily. We might not open ourselves up so easily to do what He wants. We might realize we might not be the **only** ones influencing our choices.

What can we do if Satan has control, and he has powerful people, demons, and evil spirits who are set against us?

The human condition and response

Soon the wicked will disappear,
  Though you look for them, they will be gone.
  The lowly will possess the land.
  And will live in peace and prosperity.[25]

The matter of spirituality

Since the majority of the earth's people don't believe in God, then the prevailing assumption is that we are the masters of our own destinies. Therefore, we must create systems and solutions of our own imagination, like artificial intelligence. Whatever the outcome, it is based solely on human feat and ingenuity. Or so we might believe.

I am guessing that people at the highest levels might be deceived, controlled, or both. They might make different decisions if they knew the Truth, the temporary nature of Satan's powers and rule. Or perhaps they know but prefer to get all the power, praise, adulation, and wealth right now.

That's what will cause our downfall.

Our pride and arrogance.

We are not in control. We are free to make decisions within our limited capacity, but we've never been in full control. God wants us all to know the Truth; however, Satan will do all he can to keep this hidden.

We are all susceptible to the influence of the Kingdom of Darkness. With all my beliefs and earnest desire to be devoted to the Kingdom of Light, I sometimes behave[26] in ways more consistent with the Kingdom of Darkness. This is not new or strange to any human. I am still learning always be aware that I am in a war, so I should be vigilant and alert[27].

Chapter 13: The Human Tendencies

"The Lord's light penetrates the human spirit, exposing every hidden motive." [28]

In our world, we follow man-made protocols to communicate with someone in higher authority. So, we tend to use this system as a guide to how we approach God. This need not be. In the Kingdom of Light, everyone is invited to approach God directly, no need for a middleman – we can be rich, poor, socially clumsy, uneducated - whatever you might consider may disqualify you – it doesn't matter. Just approach Him.

You don't need to know everything about Him. No one on Earth does. Not even the ruler of the Kingdom of Darkness. God made you; He knows you; He will speak to you in an understandable way. He assumes responsibility for your hearing and understanding. You only need to approach him with whatever faith or understanding you have. If you only have questions, then bring the questions. If you have fears, bring them. If you want more understanding, ask him to tell you. He knows you!

The battlefield is in our minds, for our souls.

We are wretched, all of us, in thought and in action. Since God will be our final judge, He decides what's good. And He says **He is the only** one that's good[29].

My inability to see myself deceives me into believing I am good[30]. On rare occasions, and in a limited context, when I catch a glimpse of myself, I see the depravity of my heart, and I cringe. If we could stand being brave enough to look and sustain the initial burn, we would start to heal. That's the path to cleansing, to acknowledge we need a Savior, and it's not us. We can't do it for ourselves, else it would be like using a dirty mop to clean a dirty floor.

We need the Truth about ourselves. We need to know we are depraved and cannot save ourselves. But the Creator has provided a way for us to be saved.

The solution was death. Not a physical death, but it's the death of our ego. We cannot be repaired; we must be reborn. We must sacrifice the part of us that is under the control of the Kingdom of Darkness. Death of the ego sets us free to live in this world fully as a human, and not to pretend we're God. Humans have imperfect bodies and a spirit that has been tainted. We should not hide from this truth but marvel at the solution. We die when we die to our ego and humbly accept the death of Someone else—the One who created us in the first place.

Throughout history, the Jewish people sacrificed animals to die in place of humans to make amends. Like a person who creates a will, the animal died, and the human inherited its life. It wasn't a perfect sacrifice, it was a stopgap, so they had to do it repeatedly. It was like multiple dry runs before the real thing.

Then Jesus Christ arrived on earth. **He was the perfect Human sacrifice for everyone, and because He was also God, He didn't need to die repeatedly. He set up not just a will but a new covenant, and when He died, we inherited His life. Of course, we must be part of His family to inherit.**

It was planned that He would arrive through the Jewish nation, as the Messiah. So, they expected Him to come and free them from physical

CHAPTER 13: THE HUMAN TENDENCIES

oppression. When God showed up as a humble Servant called Jesus, it didn't compute; He didn't look like what they were expecting. Today, the Jews in Judaism are still waiting for Him to come as a conquering King to get rid of oppressors. The irony is that when He does arrive the second time, He will arrive in that manner, as a conquering King. However, for those who rejected Jesus, sadly they will miss out on their inheritance.

The King is the ruler of the Kingdom of Light. Unless we are saved, we cannot enter the Kingdom of Light – not because the Light hates us, but because of our impurities. We can be purified only by believing that Jesus Christ has paid the price for our sins.

Imagine traveling toward the sun. The closer we get to it, the more likely we need to be covered in an instrument that protects us from the sun. If not, the sun will burn us up – not because the sun hates us, but because the properties that we're made of are incompatible with the sun.

The answer we are looking for today is the same as throughout history. We want a way to eradicate our physical oppression. However, that wasn't their primary need then; and it's not our primary need now. We need freedom from what really oppresses us. At the core.

As we continue to feed our fleshly desires, we'll continue to be under the control and jurisdiction of the Kingdom of Darkness that produces death. We'll continue to see death in our life, in our community, our nation, and the world. To escape from death to life in the Kingdom of Light, we must see the truth of ourselves. We are depraved, we need help, and we are not able to help ourselves. We must go through Jesus Christ as He is the only door that takes us from death to life. He is the only safety gear we can wear to stand in God's presence, by believing in Him.

The Kingdom of Darkness has been using smoke and mirrors to attract us and invite us to try all and any doors, but One Door. It is not a coincidence that the Satanic church uses an inverse cross as its symbol;

it didn't distort just any symbol but inverted (made opposite) the one that symbolizes Jesus' sacrifice. Satan opposes only one because he is the enemy of only One.

Search for Truth and human solutions

Imagine a room in darkness, and we're searching for a way out of the darkness. However, in the dark, we can't see clearly, and can't move freely. We'll end up with a different interpretation of the dark. It's like the proverbial blind man touching an elephant. Depending on where on the elephant they touch, they're convinced it is a different animal.

If we were to use light, we'd have information and clarity. We'd see the real problems and implement the right solutions.

Truth illuminates and allows us to live in freedom.

Highly intelligent people are on opposing sides on almost every issue. Some solutions are not only opposing but are mutually exclusive. That means **our intellect alone is insufficient to provide the right answers.**

There can be only one Truth. The Kingdom of Darkness has tried to land a lethal blow, by saying there's no truth. Hoping that that would end the debate, allowing Satan to continue his reign and deceive more people. However, the **Truth can be hidden or distorted, but it cannot be destroyed.**

How have we decided to settle this matter of opposing views?

We've created systems and structures to lend legitimacy to our arguments. it goes something like this, the truth is based on:
- Who has the loudest voice or who holds the microphone.
- Who has the most followers or influence.
- Who has the most wealth.
- Who is most talented.
- Who has the most power.

CHAPTER 13: THE HUMAN TENDENCIES

- Who is most educated.
- Who is most articulate.

These are human-inspired systems that the Kingdom of Darkness easily hijacks. They are unstable and unsuitable standards of measures of Truth. The Truth must be from outside of our system, or else it is as contaminated as we are.

Evil spirits may try to convince us that there is no Truth to keep us paralyzed; in contrast to Jesus, who appeared on earth to let us know Truth.

I've heard of many people who recount their personal stories of searching for the Truth and encountering Jesus. In almost all cases, they encounter Jesus, and He told them – He is the WAY, the **TRUTH,** and the LIFE.

Lucifer knows the effectiveness of the TRUTH and will do anything to keep you from the TRUTH. Once we know the Truth, we will start the journey to be free from him.

Chapter 14: The Solution to the Human Condition

"...seek first the kingdom of God...." Even the most spiritually-minded of us argue the exact opposite, saying, "But I must live; I must make a certain amount of money; I must be clothed; I must be fed." The great concern of our lives is not the kingdom of God but how we are going to take care of ourselves to live. Jesus reversed the order by telling us to get the right relationship with God first, maintaining it as the primary concern of our lives, and never to place our concern on taking care of the other things of life."
Oswald Chambers, *My Utmost for His Highest*, May 21[31]

To solve our worldwide human problem, we must go beyond our human systems to the very top, to the spiritual kingdom. To the Truth.

While science and advanced technologies have given this generation Artificial Intelligence and biotechnology, humanity has seen a degradation in the human spirit with deeper self-focus, producing moral decay which will lead to our death. It's not my intention to sound like an alarmist, but where we are today was already predicted, and where we are heading is already decided[32].

Plus, we've tried before, as we've seen throughout history. We've been trying to build a better mousetrap, and each civilization believes they have found the ultimate mousetrap. However, they all fail because they neglect to address humans' basic needs and tendencies. We are still

CHAPTER 14: THE SOLUTION TO THE HUMAN CONDITION

prone to surrender to the ego – pride, arrogance, and hate. The tools we develop only exacerbate these tendencies – which then destroy us. The only solution is represented by death on a cross—the God-man who died to give us His life.

What can you do?
It depends on whether you are a believer in Jesus Christ or not.
If you're a true believer, skip this section and move to the next.

Otherwise:

1. Be intentional about Christ. Learn about Him, then decide what you'll do about Him. Be deliberate: either believe Him or disbelieve Him. It's okay to continue to investigate Him, but don't stop pursuing Truth. Ignoring the call to decide is the same as rejecting Him, as rejecting Him is the default position, the position of the Kingdom of Darkness.
2. BELIEVE and PRAY to Jesus Christ.[33] Ask Him to send His Holy Spirit to live in you and help you live this life.
3. Read the Bible and ask God to reveal the Truth to you.
4. Establish healthy connections with other Christ-followers. This is challenging because not everyone[34] who calls themselves Christian is a true follower of Christ. But you will have help getting to the right people. Relationships are critical to our growth. They help us see our blind spots and provide opportunities to work through the darkness in us.

If you're a believer in Jesus Christ, do something different! Any positive action will do; just start moving!

Mindset change (Transform)

No matter where we are on our journey with Christ, we must continue to change. To change is to change our minds, to look more like Jesus Christ. Irrespective of how far or long we've been on this transformational journey with Him, there is **always** further to go.

Having a change of mind is not like getting an education. This learning is not to acquire power and control. It's not a "7 steps to live your best self," it's more like "How to die to my ego and allow Christ to live through me as Himself." The process and way we transform look different for everyone, as we are all original and unique. As we're minded in Psalm 32:8-9 (NLT):

> *The Lord says,*
> *"I will guide you along the best pathway for your life.*
> *I will advise you and watch over you.*
> *Do not be like a senseless horse or mule*
> *that needs a bit and bridle to keep it under control."*

Any preoccupation with the body keeps us in the realm of the Kingdom of Darkness. Christ provides for the physical body, which frees us to work with Him to build spiritual strength to do good. Do not worry about food, clothing, and shelter. He takes care of those things just as He does for the wildflowers and wild birds, and we are more valuable than those. Focus on loving Him and loving people. All people.

Loving and forgiving other humans is hard; realistically, we cannot do it without supernatural help. If we find it easy, chances are, we are **not** loving right. To love properly as Christ requires means we must die to ourselves and our desires – leaving nothing to the ego.[35]

CHAPTER 14: THE SOLUTION TO THE HUMAN CONDITION

Forgive

The 12 Disciples of Jesus were human with fears and doubts just like you and me. They got angry, were misunderstood, and made mistakes. When Jesus was arrested, they were afraid for their lives, so they ran away and hid. One even handed Him over to be arrested. Prior to that, and for over three years, they saw Him perform miracles – raise the dead, feed thousands, heal the sick, and bend nature. Despite all this evidence, they lost hope and doubted what they knew when they saw new evidence that didn't align with what they believed — Jesus' arrest and beatings made Him look weaker and less powerful than the earthly authorities. One disciple even checked out permanently.

I've done the same. I've relied on my physical talents and resources[36]. Despite what I believed, I doubted and succumbed to the Kingdom of Darkness many times. I lived as if Jesus Christ is not real, that all that's in this world is what I can see and experience through the senses.

When I remind myself and decide to live as a child of the Ruler of the Kingdom of Light, I see the difference in how I show up. However, it hasn't been consistent. Despite making mistakes, when I admit to living the way of the Kingdom of Darkness and desire to turn away from it, Jesus Christ forgives me. Every. Time. The key is for you and me to turn to Him voluntarily.

Those scared disciples became radically different after Jesus rose from the dead, ascended, and Christ's Spirit came and lived within them – they became unstoppable – joy, confidence, and boldness exuded from them. They knew death was real, but it was only a gateway, so it was not to be feared. They also knew Who lived in them, and that gave them confidence. They were finally convinced of everything Jesus taught them. **That's what I want, and that's what I want for you.**

Pray and fast

As true believers of Christ, we must **PRAY consistently** and **FAST**

regularly. If you haven't been doing this, please don't feel guilty; just start. Now.

Do you recall seeing images of Ukrainian civilians when the war started? Many were conscripted into the war and had no idea how to fight. But they showed up, volunteered, and picked up weapons (some for the first time) to fight against their enemy.

As Christ-followers, we are not fighting to win. We are fighting from a position of victory and power that Jesus Christ has given to those who believe Him. We aren't using physical weapons, as we don't fight against other human beings:

"We are not fighting against flesh-and-blood enemies, but against evil rulers and authorities of the unseen world, against mighty powers in this dark world, and against evil spirits in the heavenly places."[37]

I've noticed that some of us have laid down our **nuclear weapon of prayer** to tear down these powerful forces and instead picked up the weapons of the world to tear down social injustices. **We have been focused on winning low-hanging battles at the expense of the consequential war.**

Fasting is not as intuitive as praying. Fasting is to temporarily abstain from meeting physical needs that give pleasure or sustenance to our bodies. Generally, we abstain from food, entertainment, and such for a specific and limited time. During fasting, our posture is demonstrating to ourselves and God that we depend on the spiritual (God) and not the physical. Using the I AM Hierarchy of Needs, fasting resets our mind, soul, body, and spirit to the right priority – we exercise self-control of our physical needs to strengthen the Spirit within us.

For a more detailed and thoughtful explanation of the importance of fasting and praying, I'd recommend the YouTube video[38] *"Understanding the Power of Fasting"* by the late Dr. Myles Munroe.

CHAPTER 14: THE SOLUTION TO THE HUMAN CONDITION

Close gates to the enemy

We allow Satan and his army to influence or control us by opening portals of our souls to him. Generally, portals are open when we connect ourselves to other realms through ecstatic, traumatic, or otherworldly experiences—engagement in illicit drugs, sex, and incantations. We also open portals through less obvious means, such as malice, bitterness, unforgiveness, hate, and envy, which we tend to minimize or explain away with justification. Portals are opened when we idolize money, fame, family, reputation, ambitions, careers, jobs – anything we feel we can't live without.

On the internet, I found this definition of an idol[39], which is attributed to Tim Keller:

> *"An idol is whatever you look at and say, in your hearts, "If I have that, then I'll feel my life has meaning, then I'll know I have value, then I'll feel significance and secure.*"[40]

Let's close all portals and tear down our idols, not just the obvious ones we've labeled big sins or transgressions.

Let's live as though we're sitting in the heavenly realm beside Christ, so let's live with a pure heart because He is pure.

We are to love our enemies, do good to those who hate us, bless those who curse us, and pray for those who mistreat us. If someone slaps our cheek, we should not retaliate, and so on. If we were to start working on these, we'd take a lifetime to master them, leaving us no time to hate others.

If you've listened to anyone who has had a near-death experience, they can barely explain its completeness, purity, and beauty when they speak of heaven. We'd be undone in our own inadequacy. The purity of heaven will burn up the filth in us. If we are holding our own filth, we'll burn up. Only Jesus Christ can envelop us and protect us from such perfect awesomeness.

When we move to the heavenly realm, we'll be judged by what's in our hearts, not by the strength of our defense, the conviction of our excuses, or our passionate belief in what we think. Let's open our brokenness to Jesus; He already knows what's there.

Make disciples
"A church that doesn't disciple will eventually dissolve" [41]

It's painful to admit, but not everyone will believe Jesus Christ — no matter how polished and persuasive the evidence and arguments presented to them. As foot soldiers, we don't know who will or won't believe. But Jesus died for everyone, and the people closest to us are there for a reason. Though it doesn't flow naturally for many of us, we must tell them of Jesus Christ.

In the process, let's be patient with them. They don't know what they're doing. When Jesus was physically on earth, most people did not believe in Him. The same will happen with us.

"The Lord has blinded their eyes
and hardened their hearts—
so that their eyes cannot see,
and their hearts cannot understand,
and they cannot turn to me
and have me heal them"[42]

As C.S Lewis wrote:

> "It is right and inevitable that we should be much concerned about the salvation of those we love. But we must be careful not to expect or demand that their salvation should conform to some ready-made pattern of our own."[43]

Chapter 15: Understanding Life Versus Religious Dogma

"For the scientist who has lived by his faith in the power of reason, the story ends like a bad dream. He has scaled the mountains of ignorance, he is about to conquer the highest peak; as he pulls himself over the final rock, he is greeted by a band of theologians who have been sitting there for centuries."
Robert Jastrow, American Astronomer, NASA scientist [44]

Notice how we started discussing what we are experiencing in the world, so how have we ended up with religion? That's pointing to one of the great deceptions we face[45]. **We've transitioned our reality into religious interpretations**, then created so many religions that it has become confusing. In this mess, we've lost our connection to true reality, or at least we have a different version of reality, some even mutually exclusive.

Truth is controllable if we can convert reality into something we can put aside and label. Religion is a useful tool to this end. It has been encouraged and, in some cases, hijacked to influence or control us.

Take the Christian religion, which started with the 12 disciples of Jesus Christ. Today there are thousands of religions and denominations called "Christians," with various adherence to the worldview and teachings of Jesus Christ, some resembling Christianity only by name. This makes using the word "Christian" as useful as the word "god." The word is meaningless unless you speak with specificity.

Humans do not need a religion; we need the Truth and a way to escape the death within us. Unfortunately, some have died for knowing the Truth, others for revealing the Truth. Instead, we have sought to know where we started, where we're going, what all this means, and what's our purpose. That's knowledge, and it takes us only part of the way.

With Truth, we'll have both knowledge and wisdom. We'll see ourselves and the world as we are when we agree on that truth. Warts and all. The good, bad, and ugly. We won't attempt to solve problems that don't exist; we'd agree on true problems and work towards solving them.

Without truth:

- Histories have been written and rewritten. Consequential civilizations have been removed from our history books, and the truth about them has been erased.
- Incontrovertible physical proofs are downplayed or given an alternate storyline, such as "scientists haven't found an answer as yet."
- Wars have been fought for reasons known to few, with a people-pleasing narrative given to the masses.
- Citizens pay billions of dollars to fund projects and causes, presumably for a good cause, but later revealed to be for nefarious reasons or to benefit the gods.
- Lives are lost, and humans have been triggered to hate others because of an existential threat that doesn't exist or warrant that level of outrage.
- Humanity is being destroyed because we don't know ourselves and we don't know our enemy[46].

Religion is a way that humans connect with God. What we are seeing

CHAPTER 15: UNDERSTANDING LIFE VERSUS RELIGIOUS DOGMA

is humans developing multiple options for connecting with Him. We pick and choose religions, like how we choose where to live, which school to attend, and which gym to try out. We evaluate based on what is convenient for us. Meanwhile, we have God imploring us to come to Him. We don't need to search for Him. He knows where we are and He has already initiated contact. We need only to stop kidding and lying to ourselves, stop behaving like stubborn children and bullies - and trust Him. Humility might appear repulsive, but it is most powerful.

Shouldn't we start from God's perspective, not from our end? Shouldn't we find out who created us and the Creator's procedure for connection?

If we live as if we have only two kingdoms, we'd experience the freedom of having this binary and simple choice.

Chapter 16: Q&A Using the Two Kingdom Framework

*"What sorrow for those who say
that evil is good and good is evil,
that dark is light and light is dark,
that bitter is sweet and sweet is bitter.
What sorrow for those who are wise in their own eyes
and think themselves so clever."*[47]

What's causing us to be restless?

Removing Christ from the marketplace and institutions doesn't leave a vacuum for long. Since there are **only two** kingdoms, removing one means inviting the other. Satanic forces produce chaos, confusion, death, and mayhem[48]. That's the world we have now.

Since this war is waged in the unseen world, we ignore that world and focus instead on people. You can see the people talking, but you cannot see the spirits in and around them. The devil's army works on our thoughts. A mind that Christ does not control will think negative thoughts. Since our actions follow our thoughts and not necessarily our values, we end up with internal conflicts and external chaos.

Calls for love, tolerance, and unity do not align with our actions, as we don't have a standard to determine what these words mean or how they should look. Nonetheless, we double down on our efforts, convinced that we are "free thinking" and that our way is absolutely right and just for society.

While the war wages on the battlefields of our minds, we've lost sight of the beauty and value of humanity. We cut and carve our bodies to fill what we really need – renewed spirit. We are tearing down everything associated with our humanity – as we try to define and make sense of everything. The Kingdom of Darkness has always attempted to distort, dismember, and disembody humanity. He focuses on keeping us preoccupied with the body and not seeing what he is doing to our spirits.

Satan is after humanity and will appear to win for a while. Perhaps trans-humanism is one of his strategies to get us to cooperate willingly as he recruits. We'll give him our bodies, and he'll promise to make us like gods – supernatural - living forever without sickness and disease. However, as it was before the great Flood, the Creator of the humans must intervene.

What's happening around us?

The war escalates, and the ruler of Darkness is not as hidden as before. His gods and angels are infiltrating more spaces and places. In recent years they've been on full display on the biggest stages, with world-class choreography and marketing prowess. If you missed these events, you might search online to see the blatant display of satanic worship during:

1. 2017 CERN Opening Ceremony[49]
2. 2022 The Pharaoh's Golden Parade in Egypt
3. 2022 Commonwealth Games Opening Ceremony
4. 2023 Grammy Awards
5. 2023 Brazil Carnival

Unfortunately, many continue to see Satan and satanic displays as mere theatrics. We are distracted and fail to see what's truly happening. It's not that we should be preoccupied with his antics. We are to be courageous, focusing on the right things.

> "Satan is a powerful foe—but he is also a defeated one. The very real power of the Evil One should only ever be considered in light of the victory of the Lord Jesus. The devil has been chained by the cross of Christ. On that chain he may snarl and roar and grab for us, but nevertheless, his works will be destroyed by Christ. ..."[50]

Notice that the Satanic church adopted the upside-down cross as its symbol. They are against the symbol that points to Jesus Christ, not to other religious artifacts. The cross is an offense to Satan because it represents his annihilation. Jesus Christ's Kingdom of Light is Satan's only enemy. He's working hard to convince as many as possible that the name "Jesus Christ" should be banned and considered hateful.

They have infiltrated our homes, our schools, our communities, our businesses, and our governments – no area of human activity has been spared.

Lucifer's army is advancing, not because they are more powerful than the Kingdom of Light's, but because the army of the Kingdom of Light has been sleeping. The collective body of Christ has been infiltrated and hijacked, lulled into complacency.

The invasion of the Kingdom of Darkness can be slowed by inviting the Kingdom of Light back into these spaces. This is not to allow us to create an artificial heaven on earth, but for more opportunities to tell others the Truth. The Truth is the good news (gospel).

This is done through PRAYER to JESUS CHRIST and for HIS SPIRIT to take control and cast out the spirits of darkness. This

CHAPTER 16: Q&A USING THE TWO KINGDOM FRAMEWORK

will happen for a few years. After that period, the Kingdom of Darkness will complete its invasion, and there will be terrible times on Earth – massive earthquakes, floods, darkness, fires, and diseases. **No one knows precisely when this will happen.** The encouraging news is that the end is already written, and the Kingdom of Light wins. There is hope for humanity if only they know they have a choice.

What of solutions like the Abrahamic Family House of Worship in Saudi Arabia?

The Abrahamic Family House was opened in Saudi Arabia in 2023. It's built as an interfaith complex comprised of three religious houses of worship, representing the three populous religions that consider Abraham as their founding father. The three buildings are a church, a mosque, and a synagogue representing Catholicism ("Christianity"), Islam, and Judaism, respectively.

Years ago, a friend introduced me to the language of Esperanto. He explained that it was being developed as the universal language to promote international communication and friendship. I asked why we need Esperanto when we already have English. I can't recall his response.

The Abrahamic House is the One World Religion to accompany the One World Order. Only the Kingdom of Darkness would benefit from a single religion with no single source of reality. Religion is a human institution that provides a way to connect with God. It is easy for religion to be co-opted by the Kingdom of Darkness, and this is one example.

Any solution that directs people from seeing their sinful hearts, acknowledging they need help, and requesting help from Jesus Christ, is from the Kingdom of Darkness. These impressive structures are another attempt by the Kingdom of Darkness to misdirect people to ignore or look no further for the truth.

> "You should trust no one, and even ignore the finest saint on earth if he blocks your sight of Jesus Christ."[51]

While all three religions acknowledge Abraham as their earthly father, called by God, Jesus Christ is the only way to Father God, and He is Truth and Life. Abraham had faith, believing God would send us a Savior, even though he didn't know the earthly name, Jesus Christ.

Isn't that exclusive? Shouldn't we be more inclusive?

Yes, this is exclusive. Reality is not a game and is not subject to popular opinion or whether we agree. There are Two Kingdoms. Only two.

One Kingdom is Truth; the other is against Truth. One is for your good; the other is against you.

There is one Truth and infinite lies. If you want to live in a lie, you need only to choose **any option that is not the Truth.**

Is the Christian religion the only right one to God?

The Kingdom of Light saves people, not institutions. So, no, the "Christian" religion isn't right, but true Christ-followers are the right ones. The Christian religion has been overrun by the Kingdom of Darkness, and not everyone who says they are a Christian is a follower of Jesus Christ.

Jesus Christ is the door to get to the God of all gods – the door is not a religion, religious dogma, nation, or ideology. The door to God is a Person.

> "If we are going to be ready for Jesus Christ, we have to stop being religious. In other words, we must stop using religion as if it were some kind of a lofty lifestyle— we must be spiritually real."[52]

CHAPTER 16: Q&A USING THE TWO KINGDOM FRAMEWORK

What if I only believe in what I can see, or what scientists tell me?
It's in your control to decide what you believe. That's our responsibility as free-will humans. If you decide to accept whatever life brings you, then in the end, be prepared to accept whatever the outcome of that belief. You must be able to bet your life on it.

Isn't this a beautiful thing? The criterion for life with the God of all gods is to **believe**. Believing is one thing any human can do, irrespective of external pressure or control. It doesn't matter if you are sick, poor, rich, where you live, or what you hear around you; believing is unconstrained. Ignorance or misinformation is the enemy. Lies and deceptions hinder a free and informed belief system, so we should work to get to the Truth.

However, if you are ready to take ownership of your life and not allow others to dictate what you believe, I'd suggest you investigate further, bearing in mind that two powerful spiritual kingdoms are vying for you.

Will all Christians defy the Kingdom of Darkness?
On earth, all humans are susceptible to the influence of the Kingdom of Darkness and for various timeframes. It's not necessarily consistent. Some are under control and influence for years, months, and weeks. It may start at birth or onset at a different stage of life. We might not realize and consider Satan's thoughts as part of our personality, dispositions, family tradition, national pride, and so on.

Humans are only able to stand strong by complete reliance on Christ's Spirit and following His Word. He is the only one who loves us enough to die for us. He said what He was going to do - die for us - and will raise Himself from the dead. And He did.

What would He not do for those who believe in Him?

Chapter 17: Interpreting our World through the Two Kingdoms

Evaluating the world through the simplicity of the two Kingdoms reduces confusion in how we live.

> *"Praise the name of God forever and ever,*
> *for He has all wisdom and power.*
> *He controls the course of world events;*
> *He removes kings and sets up other kings.*
> *He gives wisdom to the wise*
> *and knowledge to the scholars.*
> *He reveals deep and mysterious things.*
> *and knows what lies hidden in darkness,*
> *though He is surrounded by light."*[53]

- If you knew the human President of the United States is President Biden, but that he is under the control of non-human powers, would you see President Biden differently? Would this help you understand why you should pray for him? Would that information help how you relate to him, not to speak ill of him?
- If you knew the human King of England is King Charles III, but the ruler of the United Kingdom is Lucifer, Kingdom of Darkness, would you pray differently for him?

CHAPTER 17: INTERPRETING OUR WORLD THROUGH THE TWO KINGDOMS

- Would that help you to see how laws, policies, and programs might not necessarily be for the people's benefit? Would it make sense if you knew they were implemented for the good of the rulers and not necessarily for humans?

If you knew that rulers, powers, and jurisdictions were being controlled or influenced by the ruler of this earth, would you react differently to what you experience? Would you respond with confidence or confusion?

Imagine a court case, and your trial isn't going in your favor. Would you be hopeful knowing there's a Higher Court? If that Higher Court is perfectly just and honest, where the judge knows you personally and your defense attorney has a 100% success rate. Wouldn't that give you a bump in your confidence?

This is not to say that every head of government and body is under the control or influence of the Kingdom of Darkness. Because of their position of control, leaders are susceptible to the Dark Kingdom. However, the Kingdom of Darkness' propensity to influence extends to everyone – you, me, our loved ones, our family, friends, coworkers, and business associates.

Not all human conflicts involve spirits.

Our environment and our sinful nature also have an influence on our decisions and actions. When threatened, I'd push the Holy Spirit aside to protect myself, then attack my "opponent." Rage, bitterness, self-deceit, and fear rolled up into pride are enough to cause death and destruction. Suppressing these feelings will reduce the carnage. However, human suppression is inadequate. Thankfully, how we show up in one moment does not define who we are. Getting up, deciding to show up differently, and making different decisions is what's expected. Jesus Christ is available to walk and help us overcome if we choose to accept Him.

His Holy Spirit helps us to bounce back, each time, every time.

We cannot fix ourselves by ourselves.

It's exhausting and impossible to transform ourselves by ourselves, so, we resort to fixing what we can by working on the external self. On our own, we can amass, nick, tuck, sculpt, carve, color, and brace, whether cosmetically or surgically, to create a new person to compensate for the broken one. Those are temporary fixes that cannot fix the root problem. The drive to fix ourselves can lead to an addiction, which leaves us even more broken. The solution is first to fix our broken spirits, and only God's Holy Spirit can fix our spirits. The result will be an adventure like none other.

How we treat humans versus spirits

- We take care of ourselves by taking care of our hearts by thinking about things that are true, right, honorable, lovely, admirable, excellent, and worthy of praise. Our physical needs are secondary as God promised to take care of those.
- For other humans, we should also take care of their hearts, irrespective of their behavior and treatment of us, we are to love them[54]. Yikes, it's tough to do!
- For Satan's spirits, we are to run from them, cast them out, and ignore them.
- For God's Spirit, we are to run to Jesus Christ. Constantly.

But this is challenging!

I know! Remember God knows we are human, and we'll sometimes

CHAPTER 17: INTERPRETING OUR WORLD THROUGH THE TWO KINGDOMS

fail - again and again[55]. He promised to forgive us every time, and I mean every time, which means He doesn't leave room for our enemy, aka the Accuser or Satan, to get his hooks into us and beat us down with guilt and shame. We will continue to experience trouble while we are in these physical bodies.

But remember, this isn't forever! We'll be on earth on average for 70 to 80 years. Considering eternity, 70-80 years is a "drop in a bucket." That's just enough time for us to decide **where** we **want** to spend our forever life and with **whom**.

The key constraint is that only the intangibles transfer from here to there. We travel so light that not even our spousal relationships travel with us. People don't marry in the next realm[56].

- If we want ourselves, we'll get the Kingdom of Darkness with our pride and ego.
- If we want earthly possessions, we get the Kingdom of Darkness, since earthly possessions are tangible. They won't travel with us.
- If we want the gifts of the Kingdom of Darkness, we get the Kingdom of Darkness, with Lucifer and his demons in a place already prepared for them.
- If we want Jesus Christ, and what He offers, then we'll get the Kingdom of Light forever with Jesus Christ in a place He is preparing for those who want Him.

It's that simple. **We'll get whatever we believe and ask for.**

Chapter 18: Notable Battles in Play

"Now the Holy Spirit tells us clearly that in the last times some will turn away from the true faith; they will follow deceptive spirits and teachings that come from demons." 1 Timothy 4:1 (NLT)[57]

Destruction of the human spirit

We hear arguments around us. The anger and indignation – how could someone think that? That is illogical! Why can't they understand? We are convinced that our ideologies and convictions are all from our brilliant minds and our pure hearts.

While humans fight other humans, those in the spiritual realm do their thing. The idea that our thoughts aren't ours or our ideologies were planted sounds ludicrous, and isn't that neglecting our individual responsibilities?

Let's consider the Two Kingdoms:

God's plan is unfolding, while the devil is trying to subvert it. The devil knows that he has limited time because God promised to destroy this earthly realm. The devil is trying to find options to survive, to defeat God.

CHAPTER 18: NOTABLE BATTLES IN PLAY

Destruction of earth

God's blueprint calls for the destruction of the present heaven and earth. Earth is the devil's domain, and *Earth's destruction is an existential threat to the devil.* He must stop God's plan. Humans have no say in any of that.

In one of his plans, the devil has influenced our leaders and followers to declare the physical earth sacred. Since God already commanded humans to take care of the environment, the devil is again giving us something we already have; in this case, our responsibility to take care of the planet.

Mass communication dictates we should double down on protecting Earth. The true reason has not been disclosed, so we have humans pitting themselves against other humans, arguing the urgency and priority of this issue.

Suggestions to reduce population growth, and deny developing countries resources to advance economically, seem counterintuitive to preserving humanity. To preserve a planet for the offspring of people you don't care for doesn't make sense. It sounds like, "Let's eradicate the current population of this region so that their descendants will have a continent in the future".

This doesn't make sense because the reasons supplied are incomplete. Like Thanos, the devil wants to destroy humanity. In the Endgame, the Earth will be destroyed. Though we don't know how the plot unfolds from here to there, we know the Avengers can't save Earth.

The human mind thinks, "Destroying the earth is bad, preserving the earth is good," – so they joined the appropriate kingdom. Elsewhere, God is building a new Earth, and this old Earth is on the chopping block!

Misinformation campaign

How the campaign is progressing:

- Christians are leaving the faith. When they sin, many walk away instead of asking for forgiveness. They didn't grasp the value of what they had or that they were following another Jesus. If you had a diamond that fell in the mud, would you throw it away?
- Distortion and trivializing the Word of God. Focus solely on the teachings of Jesus Christ and exclude His deity and the truth of human existence and future.
- The cessation of casting out demons and devils in the church or undermining of same.
- Rise of superficial teachings and diluting the Word of God.

Chapter 19: War Preparation & Assisting the War Effort

If you've been reading up to this point, you already know where my allegiance lies. The Kingdom of Darkness is our enemy and the enemy of all human beings. Don't expect me to describe how to support that war effort.

The Dark Kingdom has been waging strong offensives and is no longer working covertly. They are on our TV screens, children's classrooms, and social media feeds, parading through our streets and celebrating across the traditional podiums. Unfortunately, this dark kingdom will continue to win battles, but we should never forget – the war is already decided.

How do we know the devil and his spirits have invaded in full force?

> "And now, the giants who are produced from the spirits and flesh shall be called evil spirits on the earth. And shall live on the earth."
>
> "And these spirits shall rise up against the children of men and against the women. Because they have proceed from them in the days of slaughter and destruction.
>
> They take no food, but do not hunger or thirst. They cause offenses but are not observed." [58]

Apart from the public celebratory displays noted previously, we can also see it in others around us, and, at points of bravery, we can see it in ourselves. Yikes!

The enemy doesn't play fair and will enter us through any door we leave open to him. It doesn't matter whether we're hyper-religious or have been Christians for decades. What matters is our heart's connection to Christ. When we yield our hearts to sinful desires, it creates a hook for evil to come in, and sometimes the consequence lasts for generations. Referring to Father Gabriele's book, *"An Exorcist Tells His Story,"* [59] Vlad Savchuk mentioned five main doors through which demons enter:

1. Occult practices.
2. Repeated sinful behaviors.
3. Curses and spells.
4. Trauma.
5. Inheritance from prior generations.

We must ask God to search our hearts and show us where we have faulty thinking and deadly desires. Ask God for forgiveness and repent; ask Him to restore His Holy Spirit within us.

We are all sinners, in training as saints; we are not there yet; ask God for forgiveness. He'll never say no.

Some ways to identify humans that Satanic spirits MIGHT be controlling:

With the stresses and strains of life, people may unknowingly invite spirits into themselves. Catastrophic events over the past decades caused minor or major trauma. To cope, we might self-soothe with coping mechanisms. The coping mechanism might unknowingly include evil spirits.

CHAPTER 19: WAR PREPARATION & ASSISTING THE WAR EFFORT

These demons and evil spirits know us better than we know ourselves, they can imitate our normal behavior, but they won't get it perfectly so we might glimpse some signs. Here are some examples when you might get a glimpse of these glitches within people:

- They consistently exhibit addictive, compulsive, obsessive, or impulsive behavior.
- When scrutinized, they writhe, twist, and contort in a snake-like fashion.
- You notice they have strange, new, or different body language.
- You notice the excessive use of their tongue, protruding, snake-like.
- They exhibit intense signs of fear, despair, and panic.
- They freak out when you mention "Jesus Christ" or "Bible."
- They avoid previous social community relationships they used to enjoy.
- They want to be alone.
- They make impulsive, impassioned speeches and act contrary to their previously thoughtful beliefs.
- In their presence, you feel disconnected from them, as if they were a stranger.
- They exhibit uncharacteristic behavior with unusual quietness or excessive chatter.
- You notice a rapid deterioration in their morality and behavior. They might explain this turnaround as being enlightened or use other socially popular terminology.
- You might feel an uncharacteristic oppressive air when you are around that person.
- In extreme cases, they might have an unusually strong body odor.
- They vehemently support values that previously they adamantly opposed.
- If you challenge their new belief, their explanation is incoherent or

nonsensical.
- They get highly defensive or avoid you and your questions about their new outlook.

The Teacher's example

Mark 9:14-29 gave the account of a man who brought his son to Jesus' disciples to drive out a demon that was terrorizing his son. *The disciples failed, so the man took his son to Jesus. Jesus promptly cast out the demon and set the son free. The disciples were confused, what were they missing? Why could they not drive out the demon? Jesus said, "These are driven out only by prayer and fasting."*

Having known the power of praying <u>and</u> fasting, I've been concerned the word "fasting" is missing from verse 29, in several versions of the Bible. Jesus was speaking on how to cast out demons effectively. So, I think it's critical. The words "and fasting" while in King James Version, are **not** in other popular versions such as NLT, AMP, or ESV.

Let's grab our weapons and armor[60], fast, and pray to defend ourselves, our family and loved ones, and the entire world of humans.

All of us are on earth for a really short time, during our shift, we are to:

1. First live the life Jesus died to give us. We can do it with Christ's Spirit within us.
2. Tell others of this Good News of what God has done for humans — through Jesus Christ – who came to earth and died to give us what we most need.

Jesus has already won the victory against sin, death, Satan, gods of this earth. He said His followers will have troubles, but not to worry as He already defeated our enemies.

CHAPTER 19: WAR PREPARATION & ASSISTING THE WAR EFFORT

How to help your loved ones

- Your power is Jesus Christ. Demons will leave only by the authority of the name of Jesus Christ. Call on Jesus to cast out demons and release people.
- Get help from true believers in Jesus Christ who are familiar with driving out demons.
- Not any church will do, as many have already fallen to the enemy.
- Pray for our church leaders.

Chapter 20: The Source

Where am I getting all this stuff?
Overall, from the Bible, among other literature and life experiences.

Why the Bible?
I've found the history, guidance, and explanations outlined in the Bible to be the best explanation of the **earthly experience**. It answers the why of how I feel and see the world. It answers how I experience the world through my five senses. And it presents details of historical facts that archaeologists and other scientists are still uncovering.

Here are a few more of my reasons for believing the Bible is the inspired Word of God.

- Archaeological findings of original manuscripts, such as the Dead Sea Scrolls, agree with what's written in the **Bible**.
- From historical, non-biblical evidence that **Jesus Christ** was here on earth.
- Time is split based on God's entry onto Earth as a human being. This year is 2023 AD, which is about 2023 years since Christ arrived on Earth. Before His entry on earth, we count back from His birth, denoted, BC (Before Christ). AD – Anno Domini means in the year of our Lord. After Jesus physically left Earth, His Spirit returned to live within His people.

CHAPTER 20: THE SOURCE

- *It seems the Kingdom of Darkness is offended by the "BC" and "AD" notations since they point to Jesus Christ; so, it is working to change BC to BCE (Before Common Era) and AD to CE (Common Era).*
- **The name of Jesus Chris**t is the only effective weapon against the Kingdom of Darkness. I believe the violent opposition to this name is another proof of Jesus' authority and authenticity. If His name is ineffective, it would be easily ignored.
- **The power of the Word.** While the Bible has life-transforming principles and teachings like other ancient texts, the Bible is **more**. It gives **life** to those who are genuinely curious, or hungry – those who are asking, seeking, and knocking. It provides little to no revelation to those who approach it with disdain.
- What about other holy books? Other holy books have beneficial teachings like the Bible. But they lack a complete picture and explanation of humans. The Bible provides context for questions and answers humans need.
- The Bible is unique and uniquely inspired because the Creator had to provide instructions to His creations while knowing the Kingdom of Darkness has access to the same text. It provides information not only **in** the text but hidden truth **within** the text. Texts are interpreted and understood only with the help of Christ's Spirit. It comes alive when you accept and surrender yourself to Christ. It's a lifelong process. If you're new to this idea, what I've written might sound like hocus pocus, but it really isn't - it is complex and deep. Consequential and meaningful things are deep.
- Some religions reference the Bible and Jesus, which means they were written **after** the Bible. This gives the Bible more authority and authenticity, so I'll skip to the top of the food chain. That's the same view I have regarding other religious books, including those books of "Christian" denominations, sects, and cults. The Bible stands alone as the source and standard of truth.

The existence of a nation, called Israel.

- The account of the Jewish nation was chronicled in the first section of the Bible (confirmed by ancient manuscripts). The Bible's account, juxtaposed against other historical information, explains how these Two Kingdoms have been operating on Earth.
- Prophecies were made across centuries, like a prophecy predicting the people of Israel would scatter throughout the world, then they would return to the land and reassume their own language. The fulfillment of this prophecy during our time, 1948 AD when the nation of Israel was formed, is too compelling to ignore.
- For such a tiny nation, occupying a small strip of land, among nations with significantly larger populations and zeal to annihilate them, being able to survive handsomely, it is hard not to believe they are getting some supernatural help, as the Bible outlined.
- Since other prophecies about them have been fulfilled, I'll stick with the Book that's shown to be reliable within the earthly and spiritual realms.

Of note, **I've yet to hear or read a transformational idea that's beneficial to humans, that is not already in the Bible.**

In conclusion

In his 1927 poem, *Desiderata,* Max Ehrmann noted, "And whether or not it is clear to you, no doubt the universe is unfolding as it should. Therefore be at peace with God."[61]

We don't have to know everything about everything around us. However, we should know that the two highest kingdoms are at war, and how that war relates to us.

By default, we are all born into the Kingdom of Darkness and must spend an average of 70-80 years on Earth to decide on a Kingdom. We

CHAPTER 20: THE SOURCE

either choose the other Kingdom or keep the one we're born into. There is no third option. What we are seeing are the operations and fallout of these Kingdoms. Don't be distracted by the mayhem. Focus on what is priority and urgent.

None of us is good enough to live with the ultimate God. His standard is so high, if we hate someone, He considers it as heinous as murder. He judges not only what we do, but what we think - the condition of our hearts. If we disobey one of his laws, He considers we've broken all His laws. In a nutshell, none of us, on our own, can live right with Him.

But He had a plan, He made it possible for us to connect with Him, through Him.

God came on earth as a human, Jesus Christ. When we acknowledge the extent of our depravity and believe in Jesus Christ, God forgives us of all our sins. As Judge, He cancels all our debts, our crimes, and anything the Kingdom of Darkness has against us. We move from the Kingdom of Darkness to the Kingdom of Light. But we must decide; the Judge doesn't force us to take the plea bargain.

Choose carefully, as your life will forever depend on your choice.

I started with a quote from Yuval Harari, so it's appropriate to end with a quote. It's from Alistair Begg:

"...live knowing that the God who made you knows exactly where you are, what you're thinking, how you're feeling, and how you are trying to make sense of life as it is presented to you. Your life is an open book to God, and it's His grace alone that yields in you the realization that you are not in charge, but also that you do not need to be, for He is."[62]

APPENDIX: Status of War Operations

APPENDIX: STATUS OF WAR OPERATIONS

God's Operations	Kingdom of Light & God	Kingdom of Darkness & Satan
Human Identity *It's important that humans know the Truth – to be free.*	• God created humans in His likeness and image. Humans are like God but are not God. • Jesus Christ came in person to demonstrate what living like God looks like. That's how we should live for now. • Our relationships should reflect our status as children of God and being part of a family. • Humans were made to rule the earth, to take care of each other and the environment.	• Trick and deceive humans into believing they are gods, they were created from something obscure, and therefore they don't need God. • Promote the gods on earth and entice humans to desire those gods. • Recruit humans by meeting their legitimate desires by illegitimate means. • Convinces humans to create their own identity. • Creates their own concept of paradise. • There are no consequences to what we believe or do before we die. • Promotes being alone. Focuses on the self. Self-centeredness. • Downplay the dignity of humans.
Human to know their history, present realities, and future	• Write and preserve their history and user manual in His Word, which we call Bible. • Promote families and communities to express love in relationships. • Instruct families to observe milestones to retain identity, truth, and history. • Provide guidelines, boundaries, and laws to keep humans safe. • Outline what will happen in the future to give them hope.	• Spread doubt about the authenticity of the Bible. • Operates incognito to create doubt that he is a powerful ruler, anti-humanity, and is real and active. • Destroys families and cultures to destroy or manipulate the telling of their histories. • Makes multiple attempts to kill and destroy the lineage of Jesus: before His birth as a babe and before His second coming as King. • Uses people, powers, and scarcity to direct societies. • Promotes multiple religions, cults, systems, and powers to dilute, minimize, and undermine the Truth.

THE TWO KINGDOMS

God's Operations	Kingdom of Light & God	Kingdom of Darkness & Satan
Destroy sin and death to humans.	• Gave humans laws to keep them safe and fulfilled – morally and physically. • Sacrificed Himself and not humans to escape sin and death. • Jesus came on earth; He died and was resurrected.[i] • Won victory over the gods, demons, and evil spirits on earth and under the earth. • Jesus Christ took control over the earth and heavens.	• Convinces humans to embrace "sin" to eliminate the need for a Savior. • Lies to humans, saying that he can provide them with the ability to live forever on Earth. • Empowers rulers and powers to carry out his plans to thwart God's promise to crush him. • Convinces humans that physical death is the end of their existence. • Convinces others of a false, alternate future based on human sacrifice.
Restrain Satan, his demons, and evil spirits – forever.	• The current heaven and earth will be destroyed. • Tie up Satan and his army, first for 1000 years, then permanently.	• Builds bridges with humans to connect them to his spirits. • Hijacks the road that leads to God and seduces people away from God. • Convinces people that he does not exist. • Convinces humans that they are gods or could be, with a few tweaks or by associating with him.
Create a new heaven and earth for the ones who choose to join His family.	• Currently in process within the heavenly realm. • Next step is for this to be visible to humans.	• Connects with humans to sabotage or gather intel on what God is doing. • Deceives people by saying there is no hell, and whatever on earth is all there is. • Convinces others there is a heaven, and whatever they perceive it is, it doesn't involve Jesus Christ.

APPENDIX: STATUS OF WAR OPERATIONS

God's Operations	Kingdom of Light & God	Kingdom of Darkness & Satan
On the new earth, place the humans who have chosen Him and His kingdom, and live among them.	<ul><li>This will be the next step after the new heaven and earth are ready.</li><li>The ones who believe in Him will live on this new earth.</li><li>God will live with us.</li></ul>	<ul><li>Satan knows the earth will be destroyed, and there's nothing humans can do to stop it.</li><li>Satan will exterminate billions of humans or at least corral them to a point where they have no consciousness of and need for God.</li><li>Conducts mass brainwashing to keep people from the Truth about him, God, and salvation.</li></ul>
Provide support to humans	<ul><li>Place His Spirit in those who believe.</li><li>Enabling them to live a full and free life.</li><li>Not a trouble-free life, but a powerful life characterized by love for God, love, and care for others.</li></ul>	<ul><li>He feeds the human ego to the detriment of the spirit.</li><li>Enables his demons and spirits to terrorize and undermine God's people.</li><li>Adds to his army, using deception, terror, and enticements.</li><li>Interferes in human relations, causing conflicts, hate, and destruction to humans.</li></ul>

RESOURCES

References are based on the context noted. This does not necessarily mean I agree with everything taught or communicated by these authors or organizations. The Bible is the only book I would recommend in its entirety without qualification. While there are people I trust and admire, the only human I would promote without reservation is Jesus Christ.

Help

- 1-888-NEED-HIM Call this number if you would like to speak with someone about following Jesus Christ.
- https://www.thehopeline.com/ This is a free, virtual service for **students** and **young adults** in crisis. It offers sound advice and a safe place to connect.

Websites

- www.bible.com is a Free online Bible in many versions. A free app of the same name is also available for download.
- www.crossexamined.org Christian apologist Frank Turek and his team tackle tough questions about God and the Bible, that are posed by critical thinkers in the culture.

RESOURCES

- www.reasons.org with Dr. Hugh Ross and team
- www.pastorvlad.org with Vlad Savchuk and team

Radio

- Moody Radio is available on air and online at www.moodyradio.org

Movie

- *"Come Out in Jesus Name"* I haven't seen this documentary film, however, I've read some good reviews on it.

Books

- *"Mere Christianity"* and *"The Screwtape Letters"* by C.S Lewis
- *"The Case for Christ"* by Lee Strobel
- *"The Unseen Realm"* by Dr. Michael Heiser
- *"This Present Darkness"* by Frank E. Peretti
- The book of First Enoch. Canonized by the Ethiopian church.

YouTube Channels

- The Bible Project
- The Bible Recap
- Cross Examined
- The Gospel of Christ
- Living Waters
- Whaddo You Meme??

Notes

ACKNOWLEDGEMENT

1   **God** - Throughout this book, the word "God", with an uppercase "G", refers to Yahweh, the Creator as outlined in the Bible. He is God of all gods, King of all kings, Lord of all lords, Savior of all. "God" also refers to Jesus Christ, The Holy Spirit, Father, Son, and Holy Ghost.

2   Numbers 6:24-26

INTRODUCTION

3   **Jesus** - Jesus Christ is God who came to earth over 2000 years ago as a human, born as a human by virgin birth. His mother, Mary, was fully human. Jesus was on Earth for about 33 years. He fulfilled at least 300 prophesies (promises) that were made thousands of years prior. He was a public leader among us within the last 3 years on Earth. It ended when He was crucified. He died, and in three days, He rose from the dead. He lived among His friends, family, and community for weeks after He rose from the dead. His closest friends didn't believe, though He promised He would be raised from the dead. When He was arrested, they denied knowing Him, ran away, and hid. *No doubt, I would have done the same.* But when He arose from the dead, they were shocked and careful in verifying that it was Him. They were so convinced and convicted by what they witnessed, **nothing** and no one could deter them, not even death!

    Jesus asks us to believe Him, then live as though we believe He says who He says He is and what He has done, and He'll give us His Spirit to live in this world. This gift is immediate, but it takes a whole lifetime for Him to clean us up. But don't worry, He takes responsibility to clean us up, and while that happens, we'll trip up, but He says don't worry – no matter how badly we trip up, He'll forgive us EVERY TIME we turn back to Him. We should always TURN back to Him. Shame and condemnation are from Satan and his evil spirits; no wonder Satan is called the Accuser.

    We should all approach Jesus Christ DIRECTLY, not through anyone else or medium or as a proxy. God does not have multitiered relationships - grandchildren, cousins, great-grandniece, or any such relationship - He has children. As humans, we

NOTES

approach Jesus directly as our Savior, He saved us from the Kingdom of Darkness. **In a relationship hierarchy, the further we are from God, the easier it is to contaminate our relationship with Him.**

CHAPTER 1: HOW IT STARTED

4   https://www.youtube.com/watch?v=4Q-dOZCzBSo

CHAPTER 2: EARTHLINGS' CURRENT DILEMMA

5   Proverbs 18:14
6   Matt 7:13 You can enter God's Kingdom only through the narrow gate. The highway to hell is broad, and its gate is wide for the many who choose that way. (NLT)
7   **"god" or "gods"**
    These lowercase "g" gods are real spiritual beings we worship outside God. Any being we elevate above or prefer to, God. This could be gods of religions or gods assigned over countries and regions. They are rulers and powers of this earth.

CHAPTER 3: THE TWO KINGDOMS – STRUCTURE

8   Romans 6:16 " Don't you realize that you become the slave of whatever you choose to obey? You can be a slave to sin, which leads to death, or you can choose to obey God, which leads to righteous living."

Daniel 2:44 "During the reigns of those kings, the God of heaven will set up a kingdom that will never be destroyed or conquered. It will crush all these kingdoms into nothingness, and it will stand forever.

9   "The Trouble with X" is a short essay by C.S Lewis outlaying how difficult it is for humans to see themselves.
10 https://en.wikipedia.org/wiki/The_Emperor%27s_New_Clothes

CHAPTER 4: THE TWO KINGDOMS – SECRETS

11 Daniel 2:28 a (NLT)
12 **Satan** - Throughout, for brevity, I have used the words Lucifer, Satan, and the devil interchangeably. The key information I am conveying is that he is the highest ruler in the Kingdom of Darkness. Also, evil spirits, fallen angels, and demons describe the supernatural beings working with him. These beings have different characteristics; however, I've oversimplified and made no effort to differentiate.

CHAPTER 6: THE TWO KINGDOMS – DECLARATION OF WAR

13 Job 1:6-7

THE TWO KINGDOMS

CHAPTER 7: THE TWO KINGDOMS – HISTORY

14. The Great Flood is the worldwide flood that took place and is recorded in Genesis 6-9. Prior to the flood, the earth was watered from the ground; after the flood, we started to get rain from above, which is when we started to see rainbows. The rainbow is God's promise to never again destroy the Earth by flood.

CHAPTER 8: THE PLAN – KINGDOM OF LIGHT

15. Daniel 4:35 (NLT)

16. Isaiah 55:8 (NLT) "My thoughts are nothing like your thoughts," says the Lord. "And my ways are far beyond anything you could imagine

CHAPTER 10: THE PLAN – HUMAN EFFORTS

17. Psalm 64:6 , Proverbs 21:30

18. James 4:14-16 "How do you know what your life will be like tomorrow? Your life is like the morning fog—it's here a little while, then it's gone. What you ought to say is, "If the Lord wants us to, we will live and do this or that." Otherwise, you are boasting about your own pretentious plans, and all such boasting is evil."

CHAPTER 11: THE WAR OPERATION

19. Psalm 2:1-6

20. 1 Corinthians 2:7-8 "The wisdom we speak of is the mystery of God—His plan that was previously hidden, even though He made it for our ultimate glory before the world began. But the rulers of this world have not understood it; if they had, they would not have crucified our glorious Lord."

21. Exodus 7:22a "But again the magicians of Egypt used their magic, and they, too, turned water into blood."

CHAPTER 12: HUMAN SYSTEMS AND OPERATIONS

22. Psalm 8:4

23. 2 Corinthians 4:4a (NLT) "Satan, who is the god of this world, has blinded the minds of those who don't believe. They are unable to see the glorious light of the Good News."

24. https://www.youtube.com/shorts/2_LRlmfPj1w

25. Psalm 37:10-11 (NLT)

26. Romans 7:21-23,25 (NLT) "When I want to do what is right, I inevitably do what is wrong. I love God's law with all my heart. But there is another power within me

NOTES

that is at war with my mind. This power makes me a slave to the sin that is still within me...... Thank God! The answer is in Jesus Christ our Lord."

27 1 Peter 5:8 (NLT) Stay alert! Watch out for your great enemy, the devil. He prowls around like a roaring lion, looking for someone to devour.

CHAPTER 13: THE HUMAN TENDENCIES

28 Proverbs 20:27
29 Mark 10:18, Psalm 53:1
30 See C.S Lewis' short essay "The Trouble with X"

CHAPTER 14: THE SOLUTION TO THE HUMAN CONDITION

31 Matthew 6:33 (KJV) "But seek ye first the Kingdom of God, and His righteousness, and all these things shall be added unto you."
32 The Book of Revelations
33 John 14:6: Jesus told him, "I am the way, the truth, and the life. No one can come to the Father except through me.
34 Matthew 7:21 "Not everyone who calls out to me, 'Lord! Lord!' will enter the Kingdom of Heaven. Only those who actually do the will of my Father in heaven will enter."
35 Romans 13:8 (KJV) "Owe no man anything, but to love one another."
36 Galatians 5:16b (NLT)"Let the Holy Spirit guide your lives. Then you won't be doing what your sinful nature craves."
37 Ephesians 6:12 (NLT)
38 Dr. Myles Munroe- Understanding the Power of Fasting: https://www.youtube.com/watch?v=53nuAnFzIEE
39 Idols
    Idols are objects that we worship. They can be spiritual or physical. They could be gods we've created in our hearts by devotion, dependence, and energy – such as relationships, money, affirmations, work, and pleasure.
40 Reference link https://www.kevinhalloran.net/tim-kellers-definition-of-idolatry/
    Tim Keller on pages xvii and xviii of *Counterfeit Gods: The Empty Promises of Money, Sex, and Power, and the Only Hope that Matters*
41 CJ Johnson, Sermon: Bad Advice – Just be Yourself, 1/15/2022.
42 John 12:40
43 C.S Lewis, *The Quotable Lewis*, Martindale & Root, 1990 - Evangelism

CHAPTER 15: UNDERSTANDING LIFE VERSUS RELIGIOUS DOGMA

44   Robert Jastrow, *God and the Astronomers*, referenced on goodreads.com

45   2 Thess. 2:10 (NLT) "He will use every kind of deception to fool those on their way to destruction, because they refuse to love and accept the truth that would save them.

46   Hosea 4:6a (KJV) "My people are destroyed for lack of knowledge."

CHAPTER 16: Q&A USING THE TWO KINGDOM FRAMEWORK

47   Isaiah 5:20-21

48   Romans 1:24-26 So God abandoned them to do whatever shameful things their hearts desired. As a result, they did vile and degrading things with each other's bodies. They traded the truth about God for a lie. So, they worshiped and served the things God created instead of the Creator himself."

49   https://www.youtube.com/watch?v=TlG5WR_TeaY

50   Alistair Begg: Truth for Life, e-newsletter published, 3/14/2023.

51   Oswald Chambers, "*My Utmost for His Highest*", March 29, Edited by James Reimann

52   Oswald Chambers, "*My Utmost for His Highest*", March 29, , Edited by James Reimann

CHAPTER 17: INTERPRETING OUR WORLD THROUGH THE TWO KINGDOMS

53   Daniel 2:20-22 (NLT)

54   Luke 6:27-28 (NLT): "But to you who are willing to listen, I say, love your enemies! Do good to those who hate you. Bless those who curse you. Pray for those who hurt you."

55   1 John 5:18 (NLT): "We know that God's children do not make a practice of sinning, for God's Son holds them securely, and the evil one cannot touch them."

56   Luke 20:34-35: "Marriage is for people here on earth. But in the age to come, those worthy of being raised from the dead will neither marry nor be given in marriage."

CHAPTER 18: NOTABLE BATTLES IN PLAY

57   1 Timothy 4:1

CHAPTER 19: WAR PREPARATION & ASSISTING THE WAR EFFORT

58   I Enoch 15:8-9a, 11-12, *The Books of Enoch*, page 43, Lumpkin 2011

59   Vlad Savchuk https://www.youtube.com/shorts/FdnI65Lm_AY ref: "*An Exorcist Tells His Story.*"

60   Ephesians 6: 13-18 The armor of God

CHAPTER 20: THE SOURCE

61 www.desiderata.com

62 Alistair Begg Devotional, Truth for Life, 6/12/2023 *"The Same Old Routine"*

APPENDIX: STATUS OF WAR OPERATIONS

63 <u>Genesis 1:28</u> (KJV) "And God blessed them, and God said unto them, be fruitful, and multiply, and replenish the earth, and subdue it: and have dominion over the fish of the sea, and over the fowl of the air, and over every living thing that moveth upon the earth"

<u>2 Timothy 3: 16-17</u> (NLT) "All Scripture is inspired by God and is useful to teach us what is true and to make us realize what is wrong in our lives. It corrects us when we are wrong and teaches us to do what is right. God uses it to prepare and equip His people to do every good work."

<u>John 14:6</u> (NLT) "Jesus told him, *"I am the Way, the Truth, and the* Life. No one can come to *the* Father except through Me."

About the Author

Jennifer is a child of God and a follower of Jesus Christ. She has worked as an Information Technology executive and professional for over 30 years.

Jennifer was born in Jamaica, where she started her education and career in IT. In the early 2000s, a Microsoft partner recruited her to work in the US, implementing software solutions for corporate businesses. In 2021 she started her own company, delivering coaching and mentoring services to software consultants. Jennifer writes monthly blogs to spread awareness of her business. However, she soon discovered her blogs were not the typical technology blog, "How to... ". She found herself writing aspirational topics that spoke to one's core beliefs and not just knowledge and behavior. This bent to the spiritual is one factor that led her to write this book.

Jennifer is not a theologian and has served only as a layperson.

You can connect with me on:
- https://www.jenniferstarns.com

Made in the USA
Monee, IL
23 July 2023

39692133R00069